P9-EGB-809

Peer Reviews in Software

Addison-Wesley Information Technology Series
Capers Jones and David S. Linthicum, Consulting Editors

The information technology (IT) industry is in the public eye now more than ever before because of a number of major issues in which software technology and national policies are closely related. As the use of software expands, there is a continuing need for business and software professionals to stay current with the state of the art in software methodologies and technologies. The goal of the Addison-Wesley Information Technology Series is to cover any and all topics that affect the IT community: These books illustrate and explore how information technology can be aligned with business practices to achieve business goals and support business imperatives. Addison-Wesley has created this innovative series to empower you with the benefits of the industry experts' experience.

For more information point your browser to http://www.awl.com/cseng/series/it/

Sid Adelman, Larissa Terpeluk Moss, *Data Warehouse Project Management.* ISBN: 0-201-61635-1

Wayne Applehans, Alden Globe, and Greg Laugero, *Managing Knowledge: A Practical Web-Based Approach.* ISBN: 0-201-43315-X

Michael H. Brackett, *Data Resource Quality: Turning Bad Habits into Good Practices.* ISBN: 0-201-71306-3

Frank Coyle, *Wireless Web: A Manager's Guide.* ISBN: 0-201-72217-8

James Craig and Dawn Jutla, *e-Business Readiness: A Customer-Focused Framework.* ISBN: 0-201-71006-4

Gregory C. Dennis and James R. Rubin, *Mission-Critical Java™ Project Management: Business Strategies, Applications, and Development.* ISBN: 0-201-32573-X

Kevin Dick, *XML: A Manager's Guide.* ISBN: 0-201-43335-4

Jill Dyché, *e-Data: Turning Data into Information with Data Warehousing.* ISBN: 0-201-65780-5

Jill Dyché, *The CRM Handbook: A Business Guide to Customer Relationship Management.* ISBN: 0-201-73062-6

Patricia L. Ferdinandi, *A Requirements Pattern: Succeeding in the Internet Economy.* ISBN: 0-201-73826-0

Dr. Nick V. Flor, *Web Business Engineering: Using Offline Activites to Drive Internet Strategies.* ISBN: 0-201-60468-X

David Garmus and David Herron, *Function Point Analysis: Measurement Practices for Successful Software Projects.* ISBN: 0-201-69944-3

John Harney, *Application Service Providers (ASPs): A Manager's Guide.* ISBN: 0-201-72659-9

Capers Jones, *Software Assessments, Benchmarks, and Best Practices.* ISBN: 0-201-48542-7

Capers Jones, *The Year 2000 Software Problem: Quantifying the Costs and Assessing the Consequences.* ISBN: 0-201-30964-5

Ravi Kalakota and Marcia Robinson, *e-Business 2.0: Roadmap for Success.* ISBN: 0-201-72165-1

David S. Linthicum, *B2B Application Integration: e-Business-Enable Your Enterprise.* ISBN: 0-201-70936-8

Sergio Lozinsky, *Enterprise-Wide Software Solutions: Integration Strategies and Practices.* ISBN: 0-201-30971-8

Joanne Neidorf and Robin Neidorf, *e-Merchant: Retail Strategies for e-Commerce.* ISBN: 0-201-72169-4

Patrick O'Beirne, *Managing the Euro in Information Systems: Strategies for Successful Changeover.* ISBN: 0-201-60482-5

Bud Porter-Roth, *Request for Proposal: A Guide to Effective RFP Development,* ISBN: 0-201-77575-1

Mai-lan Tomsen, *Killer Content: Strategies for Web Content and E-Commerce.* ISBN: 0-201-65786-4

Karl E. Wiegers, *Peer Reviews in Software: A Practical Guide.* ISBN: 0-201-73485-0

Bill Wiley, *Essential System Requirements: A Practical Guide to Event-Driven Methods.* ISBN: 0-201-61606-8

Ralph R. Young, *Effective Requirements Practices.* ISBN: 0-201-70912-0

Bill Zoellick, *CyberRegs: A Business Guide to Web Property, Privacy, and Patents.* ISBN: 0-201-72230-5

Bill Zoellick, *Web Engagement: Connecting to Customers in e-Business.* ISBN: 0-201-65766-X

Peer Reviews in Software

A Practical Guide

Karl E. Wiegers

Addison-Wesley

Boston • San Francisco • New York • Toronto • Montreal
London • Munich • Paris • Madrid
Capetown • Sydney • Tokyo • Singapore • Mexico City

Many of the designations used by manufacturers and sellers to distinguish their products are claimed as trademarks. Where those designations appear in this book, and Addison-Wesley, Inc. was aware of a trademark claim, the designations have been printed with initial capital letters or in all capitals.

The author and publisher have taken care in the preparation of this book, but make no expressed or implied warranty of any kind and assume no responsibility for errors or omissions. No liability is assumed for incidental or consequential damages in connection with or arising out of the use of the information or programs contained herein.

The publisher offers discounts on this book when ordered in quantity for special sales. For more information, please contact:

Pearson Education Corporate Sales Division
201 W. 103rd Street
Indianapolis, IN 46290
(800) 428-5331
corpsales@pearsoned.com

Visit AW on the Web: www.aw.com/cseng/

Library of Congress Cataloging-in-Publication Data

Wiegers, Karl Eugene, 1953–
    Peer reviews in software : a practical guide / Karl E. Wiegers.
        p. cm.—(The Addison-Wesley information technology series)
    Includes bibliographical references and index.
    ISBN 0-201-73485-0
    1. Computer software—Quality control. 2. Peer review. I. Title. II. Series.

QA76.76.Q35 W54 2002
005.1—dc21
                                            2001045902

Copyright © 2002 by Karl E. Wiegers

All rights reserved. No part of this publication may be reproduced, stored in a retrieval system, or transmitted, in any form, or by any means, electronic, mechanical, photocopying, recording, or otherwise, without the prior consent of the publisher. Printed in the United States of America. Published simultaneously in Canada.

For information on obtaining permission for use of material from this work, please submit a written request to:

Pearson Education, Inc.
Rights and Contracts Department
75 Arlington Street, Suite 300
Boston, MA 02116
Fax: (617) 848-7047

0-201-73485-0
Text printed on recycled paper
1 2 3 4 5 6 7 8 9 10—ML—0504030201
First printing, November 2001

Contents

Preface

No matter how skilled or experienced I am as a software developer, requirements writer, project planner, test engineer, or book author, I'm going to make mistakes. There's nothing wrong with making mistakes; it's part of what makes me human. But because I err, it makes sense to catch the errors early, before they become difficult to find and expensive to correct.

Finding my own errors is often hard because I am too close to the work. Many years ago I learned the value of having some colleagues look over my work and point out my mistakes. I always feel a bit sheepish when they do, but I prefer to have them find the mistakes now than to have customers find them much later. Such examinations are called *peer reviews*. There are several different types of peer reviews, including inspections, walkthroughs, and others. Most of the points I make in this book apply to any activity in which someone other than the creator of a work product examines it in order to improve its quality.

I began performing software peer reviews in 1987; today I would never consider a work product complete unless someone else has carefully examined it. You might never find all of the errors, but with help from other people you will find many more than you possibly can on your own. The manuscript for this book and my previous books all underwent extensive peer review, which contributed immeasurably to their quality.

My Objectives

There is no "one true way" to conduct a peer review, so the principal goal of this book is to help you effectively perform appropriate reviews of deliverables that people in your organization create. I also address the cultural and practical aspects of implementing an effective peer review program in a software organization. Inspection is emphasized as the most formal and effective type of peer review, but I also describe several other methods that span a spectrum of formality and rigor. Many references point you to the extensive literature on software reviews and inspections.

Inspection is both one of the great success stories of software development and something of a failure. It's a grand success because it works! Since Michael Fagan developed it at IBM in the 1970s, inspection has become one of the most powerful methods available for finding software errors. You don't have to just take my word for it, either. Experiences cited from the software literature describe how inspections have improved the productivity of many software organizations and the quality of their products. However, only a fraction of the software development community understands the inspection process and even fewer people practice inspections properly and effectively. To help you implement inspections and other peer reviews in your team, this book emphasizes pragmatic approaches that any organization can apply.

Several process assets that can jumpstart your peer review program are available from the Web site that accompanies this book. Find it by going to one of these locations:

http://www.processimpact.com/pr_goodies.shtml
http://www.awl.com/cseng/

These resources include review forms, defect checklists, a sample peer review process description, spreadsheets for collecting inspection data, sources of training on inspections, and more, as described in Appendix B. You are welcome to download these documents and adapt them to meet your own needs. Please send your comments and suggestions to me at kwiegers@acm.org. Feedback on how well you were able to make peer reviews work in your team is also welcome.

Intended Audience

The material presented here will be useful to people performing many project functions, including:

- Work product authors, including analysts, designers, programmers, maintainers, test engineers, project managers, marketing staff, product managers, technical writers, and process developers
- Work product evaluators, including quality engineers, customer representatives, customer service staff, and all those listed as authors
- Process improvement leaders
- Managers of any of these individuals, who need to know how to instill peer reviews into their cultures and also should have their own deliverables reviewed

This book will help people who realize that their software product's quality falls short of their goals and those who want to tune up their current review practices, establish and maintain good communications on their projects, or ship high-quality software on schedule. Organizations that are using the Capability Maturity Model for Software or the CMMI for Systems Engineering/Software Engineering will find the book valuable, because peer reviews are components of those process improvement frameworks (see Appendix A).

The techniques described here are not limited to the deliverables and documents created on software projects. Indeed, you can apply them to technical work products from any engineering project, including design specifications, schematics, assembly instructions, and user manuals. Any business that has documented task procedures or quality control processes will find that careful peer review will discover errors the author simply cannot find on his own.

Reading Suggestions

To gain a detailed understanding of peer reviews in general and inspections in particular, you can simply read the book from front to back. The cultural and social aspects of peer reviews are discussed in Chapters 1 and 2. Chapter 3 provides an overview of several different types of reviews and suggests when each is appropriate. Chapters 4 through 8 address the nuts and bolts of inspection, while Chapter 9 describes important inspection data items and metrics. If you're attempting to implement a successful review program in an organization, focus on Chapters 10 and 11. For suggestions on ways to deal with special review challenges, such as large work products or distributed development teams, see Chapter 12. Refer to the Glossary for definitions of many terms used in the book.

Acknowledgments

What could be a more appropriate candidate for peer review than a book on peer reviews? My stalwart reviewers for this book were Sandy Browning, Tim Bueter, Rodger Drabick, Chris Fahlbusch, Lynda Fleming, Kathy Getz, Robin Goldsmith, Ellen Gottesdiener, Brian Lawrence, Karen Mattheessen, Mark Paulk, John Pustaver, Jenny Stuart, Troy Taft, Don Thresh, Scott Whitmire, Nancy Willer, and Ralph Young. They offered valuable improvement suggestions for nearly every chapter. I also appreciate those who commented on selected sections, including Brad Appleton, James Bach, Mike Dahlhausen, Zarrin Ghaemi, Tom Gilb, Bob Glass, Tammy Hoganson, Claude Laporte, Gloria Leman, Ron Radice, Phil Recchio, Kathy Rhode, Erik Simmons, and Dan Wall.

I'm grateful to Brian Lawrence for generously sharing his excellent treatise "Effective Peer Reviews" with me and to Kathy Rhode for relating her inspection experiences. Thanks also to David Gelperin for suggesting that the world needed a new book on software peer reviews and for imparting his wisdom regarding inspections.

It was a pleasure working with acquisitions editor Deborah Lafferty and production coordinator Patrick Peterson of Addison-Wesley. Malinda McCain did a fine job of editing the initial manuscript into final form, and Stratford Publishing Services rendered my simple sketches into effective figures.

And once again: thank you for your support and patience, Chris. They get easier with practice.

About the Author

Karl E. Wiegers is the Principal Consultant with Process Impact, a software process consulting and education company in Portland, Oregon. His interests include software quality engineering, requirements engineering, project management, risk management, metrics, and software process improvement. Previously, he spent eighteen years at Eastman Kodak Company, where he held positions as a photographic research scientist, software developer, software manager, and software process and quality improvement leader. Karl received a B.S. degree in chemistry from Boise State College and M.S. and Ph.D. degrees in organic chemistry from the University of Illinois. He is a member of the IEEE, IEEE Computer Society, and ACM.

Karl is the author of the books *Software Requirements* (Microsoft Press, 1999) and *Creating a Software Engineering Culture* (Dorset House Publishing, 1996), both of which won Productivity Awards from *Software Development* magazine. He has also written more than 140 articles on many aspects of computing, chemistry, and military history. Karl has served as a member of the Editorial Board for *IEEE Software* magazine and as a contributing editor for *Software Development* magazine. He is a frequent speaker at software conferences and professional society meetings. When not in front of the keyboard, Karl enjoys cooking, wine, studying military history, riding his Suzuki VX800 motorcycle, and playing his Gibson Les Paul and Fender Stratocaster guitars.

CHAPTER ONE

The Quality Challenge

"Hey, Maria, do you have a minute? I can't find a silly little bug in this program. Can you take a look at this code for me, please?"

"Sure, Phil. What's it doing wrong?"

"It's not aligning these images correctly. They're all supposed to be left-aligned, but each one is indented farther in. I'm pretty sure the problem is in the DisplayImage function, but I've been looking at it for 15 minutes and I just can't see anything wrong."

"Hmmm, let's see here. It looks like . . ." [mutter, mutter, mutter] "No, that part looks fine. But look at the top of this loop." [Maria points to the screen.] "I think this parenthesis is in the wrong place. If you move the index variable outside that paren, I don't think the images will be stairstepped any more."

Phil smacks his forehead with his palm. "You're right! Thanks a lot, Maria. I can't believe I didn't see that."

"No problem, Phil. I'm glad to help."

Most programmers have asked their colleagues to help them find elusive problems in their code. Often you are too close to your own work to spot errors you've made. As you study the code, your brain just recites what you created earlier (or what you intended to create) because you're following the same reasoning you used when you made the mistake. You need a fresh perspective—a pair of eyes that hasn't seen the code before and a brain that thinks in a different way.

Looking Over the Shoulder

In a *peer review,* someone other than the author of a work product examines that product to find defects and identify improvement opportunities. A *defect* (also known as a bug or a fault) is a condition in a software work product that would cause the software to produce an unsatisfactory or unexpected result. Phil asked Maria to conduct a short code review because he knew he was stuck, and Maria was able to get him unstuck after studying the problem code for just a few moments. Even if your organization adopts a formal peer review process, continue to rely on the kindness of your colleagues through these quick, ad hoc reviews.

People conduct various types of project reviews besides peer reviews intended to discover defects; see Table 1–1 for some examples. Although all of these reviews contribute to successful project execution and might involve "peers" of the author, this book focuses on peer reviews whose primary objective is to improve product quality.

Table 1–1. Types of Project Reviews

Review Type	*Purpose*
Educational review	Bring other stakeholders up to speed on technical topics pertinent to the project
Management, readiness, or gate review	Provide information to senior managers so they can decide to release a product, continue (or cancel) a development project, approve (or reject) a proposal, change project scope, adjust resources, or alter commitments
Peer review	Look for defects and improvement opportunities in a work product
Post-project review	Reflect on a recently completed project or phase to learn lessons for future projects
Status review	Update the project manager and other team members on progress toward milestones, problems encountered, and risks identified or controlled

The term "peer review" is sometimes misinterpreted to mean that people are evaluating a coworker's performance. Not so—the point of any peer review is to critique a work product, not the individual who created it. Peer review has long been a fundamental component of scientific and engineering endeavor. A scientist's colleagues can judge whether a body of work meets professional standards and can look for errors in experiment or equipment design, data gathering, or results analysis. Scientific results are not considered valid until they've passed the peer review gauntlet. That's not a bad philosophy for software development, either. As described in Appendix A, several widely used process-improvement frameworks identify peer reviews as a key practice an organization must master to improve its software engineering capability.

When I use the term "review" or "peer review," I'm referring to the general activity of any software peer review, without regard to precisely how it is conducted. The terms "review," "inspection," and "walkthrough" sometimes are used interchangeably, but they represent different methods for performing peer reviews. Chapter 3 describes a spectrum of peer reviews that range from the very informal (like Phil and Maria's over-the-shoulder experience) to the highly systematic and disciplined process of inspection. Chapter 3 also suggests appropriate review techniques that will satisfy specific project objectives.

The goal of reviews is not only to catch errors and gather improvement suggestions, but also to help authors create better work products in the future. I have learned something from every review in which I've participated as either an author or a reviewer. The benefits I have personally experienced through peer reviews are so compelling that I would never work in an organization that did not perform them.

Quality Isn't Quite Free

Managers, developers, and customers sometimes oppose peer reviews because they believe reviews will cost too much and slow down the project. In reality, reviews don't slow the project—defects do. Anyone who has suffered through the frantic test-and-debug sessions that delay shipping of a finished product understands the high cost of bugs found late in the game. Reviews are a waste of time only if your work products do not contain defects the reviews could find.

Perhaps you've heard that quality is free (Crosby 1979). This is a bit oversimplified. "Quality is free" means your investment in building quality into a product is more than repaid by reducing the costs of late-stage defect correction and customer-reported problems. One way to think about the impact of defects on your project and product is to consider the *cost of quality.* The cost of quality includes the time and money you spend in several categories:

- *External product failure,* including dealing with customer-reported defects, making code patches or unplanned releases available, and implementing missing functionality
- *Internal product failure,* such as fixing bugs found through testing or by peer review prior to product release, defect management, rebuilding flawed components, and retesting modified components
- *Quality appraisal,* such as performing reviews or testing to find defects, and collecting and analyzing quality metrics
- *Defect prevention,* including training developers, analyzing the root causes of defects, and developing improved engineering and quality processes

Rework—time spent redoing something you thought was already done—is a major contributor to a project's cost of quality. Rework wreaks havoc on your software development productivity, as many small corrections eat up hours of effort. Organizations that measure rework find that it can consume 40 to 60 percent of the total development effort (C. Jones 1986; Cooper and Mullen 1993; Haley 1996; Wheeler, Brykczynski, and Meeson Jr. 1996b). Although reviews consume resources and hence are not free, the time you spend on them can reduce the amount of rework you have to do later in the project. That avoided rework time is available for doing the development work that provides value to your customers and your business.

Investing in peer reviews shifts some of your organization's cost of quality from expensive, late-stage rework to early defect detection and—even better— defect avoidance as work product authors learn how to do a better job. The defects are there whether you look for them or not; it's just a question of how much it will cost to fix them when they finally raise their ugly heads. As one example, Raytheon Electronic Systems reduced its rework level from 41 percent of total project cost to 20 percent in two years, in large part by implementing an inspection program (Haley 1996). Raytheon also reduced the effort needed to fix code problems found during integration by 80 percent and cut its retesting effort in half. Reviews also reveal ways to improve your development processes and improve your organization's efficiency through defect prevention, a powerful strategic benefit. It is cheaper to prevent defects than to remove them after you have completed implementation or shipped the product.

Shifting defect detection to the early stages of product development has a huge potential payoff because of the high cost of fixing defects found late in the development cycle or after release. The Space Shuttle Onboard Software project measured the relative cost of correcting a design or code defect as $1 if it was found during an inspection, $13 during system test, and $92 after delivery (Paulk et al. 1995). Other studies have shown that fixing a requirements-related defect reported by a customer can cost 68 to 110 times as much as finding and fixing such a defect during requirements development (Boehm 1981; Grady 1999).

One of my consulting clients, a telecommunications company, spends an average of $200 to find and fix a defect by inspection, compared to an average of $4,200 to correct each customer-reported defect. The amplification factor is less severe for small, noncritical systems, but it is never zero (Boehm and Basili 2001). You can also use reviews to evaluate other aspects of product quality, such as reliability, robustness, maintainability, and testability. If the cost of establishing and sustaining a review program, training your team, and holding reviews (the investment) is less than what you save through reduced rework and enhanced customer satisfaction (the return), you come out ahead.

Every project team must balance its investment in initial product quality against its other business success objectives, such as time to market, feature content, and long-term maintenance costs. A common perception is that peer reviews are a luxury that schedule-driven projects cannot afford. Yes, reviews take time, but whether they take *too much* time is a business issue. Intelligently applied, peer reviews can actually shorten product development schedules by letting you bypass some testing stages (Weller 1993).

Sometimes management or marketing decides not to perform quality practices that might have long-term benefits in favor of releasing a "good enough" product more quickly. They make a business tradeoff between trying to meet aggressive delivery schedules and devoting additional future resources to fixing problems. Such decisions must be based on an informed risk assessment of the cost of quality variables and the possible business implications. If managers recognize the need for quality over the long term, they will build time for reviews into project schedules.

In the Internet world, time to market is often viewed as paramount. However, the cost of poor quality on e-commerce projects includes business opportunities lost because of defective products. "Good enough" quality means the product must be good enough for the consumer to willingly use it more than once. I read a review (yet a different definition of "review") of a new flight simulation game that said, "The software is sadly unfinished, however, and terrible bugs, documentation discrepancies and disrupted functionality plague this title" (Dy 2001). Perhaps it would have been better for the developing company to release a higher quality product a bit later and in an improved condition that avoided such negative reviews. As another example, I once ordered new checks for my checking account from a supplier on the Internet. When I inquired a week later, the supplier had no record of my order. The Web site had confirmed acceptance of my order, so I can only conclude that a software defect led to an inconvenience for the customer (me). I won't use that e-commerce service again.

Reviews might not find all the defects lurking in your products, but they should be part of your defect-detection arsenal. There is a good chance that spending time on peer reviews will actually speed your product to market, not delay it. You need to estimate the likelihood of undetected bugs remaining in each product and assess their possible impact so you can decide how much to invest in quality. Following are some examples of questions to ask yourself from a business perspective:

- What would a two-hour outage of a telecommunications system cost?
- What would it cost to lose a spacecraft because of a defect that a review should have caught?
- How would a bad product review or negative comments in a discussion group affect sales of your new computer game or your future titles?
- How much would it hurt you to launch your revamped corporate Web site one week later than planned versus launching on schedule with a major security defect?
- What is your liability exposure from defective code embedded in an automobile safety device, such as an air bag system?

Justifying Peer Reviews

Although no one can predict exactly what return on investment (ROI) a specific organization will achieve from any new practice, many companies have described impressive returns from inspections. Little data is available regarding less formal reviews, because they typically do not include data collection. Until you accumulate enough data to demonstrate your own ROI, a bit of a leap of faith is needed. Managers and technical practitioners should respect the body of literature on inspections and be willing to try them, based on decades of published experience. Following are some sample benefits that inspection practitioners have obtained:

- Hewlett-Packard's inspection program measured a return on investment of 10 to 1, saving an estimated $21.4 million per year. Holding design inspections on one project reduced the time to market by 1.8 months (Grady and Van Slack 1994).
- At AT&T Bell Laboratories, inspection reduced the cost of finding errors by a factor of ten. Inspections also contributed to a ten-fold improvement in quality and a 14 percent increase in productivity (Humphrey 1989).
- Inspecting 2.5 million lines of real-time code at Bell Northern Research prevented an average of 33 hours of maintenance effort per defect discovered. Finding defects through inspection was two to four times faster than revealing them through testing (Russell 1991).
- IBM reported that each hour of inspection saved 20 hours of testing and 82 hours of rework effort needed if the defects found by inspection had remained in the released product (Holland 1999).
- During the first five years of a broad inspection program, Primark Investment Management Services enjoyed a total savings of nearly 30,000 labor hours of effort. Primark also saw a five-fold decrease in product errors reported per customer per year (Holland 1999).
- At Imperial Chemical Industries, the cost of maintaining a portfolio of about 400 programs that had been inspected was one-tenth the cost per line of code of maintaining a similar set of 400 uninspected programs (Gilb and Graham 1993).
- Litton Data Systems invested just 3 percent of its total project effort in inspections and reduced the number of errors found during system integration and system testing by 30 percent. Design and code inspections cut product integration effort in half (Madachy 1995).

You should judge cost-effectiveness by how many hours of work your team saves through peer reviews, not by how many bugs they uncover. Chapter 9 describes a process for estimating the ROI from reviews in a specific organization.

Keep in mind that the ROI will be zero if poorly executed reviews don't find bugs, if the bugs they do reveal aren't corrected, or if your team doesn't actually hold reviews after you invest in peer review training and process development.

Peer reviews yield additional benefits that are difficult to quantify. One is the knowledge that individuals gain from having other people provide feedback on their work. Reviews spread product, project, and technical knowledge among the team members, supplementing formal communication and training mechanisms. They help the team establish shared expectations, they reveal assumptions, and they create a shared understanding of technical work products. Reviews help practitioners build products that are simple and understandable, which reduces maintenance and enhancement costs. As Donald Knuth pointed out, programs should be written so that both people and compilers can read them (Knuth 1992). Developers are more careful to write well-structured, documented, high-quality programs when they know that other people will be checking them.

Reviews help build a collaborative mindset, with team members willing to share their knowledge, learn from each other, and contribute to the quality of each system component. Developers learn about application components besides their own, which provides a clearer context for everyone's work. Cross-training and knowledge exchange through peer reviews reduce the risk of losing critical information in these days of software industry job-hopping. The many rewards of peer reviews nearly always exceed their cost.

Peer Reviews, Testing, and Quality Tools

Quality control activities determine whether a product conforms to its requirements, specifications, or pertinent standards. Nonconformances constitute defects. Performing quality control within the development process (verification) is more efficient than looking for errors after the product has been completed (validation). Peer review is a verification method you can use to improve work products *before* they are completed. Most forms of dynamic test execution reveal places where the quality is deficient only after a software product or component is complete. Testing cannot demonstrate whether a product complies with standards, either.

The effective software practitioner has a rich tool kit of quality techniques. In addition to the traditional testing practices and peer reviews, many software quality tools are commercially available. These include static analyzers that examine source code for possible errors and tools that look for run-time problems such as memory leaks and pointer problems. Developers sometimes question the value of manual code reviews when so many other quality tools are available, but these tools and practices complement each other. Code analyzers can find subtle syntax errors and likely problem areas such as uninitialized variables that the human eye might not see, but they won't detect logic errors in the implementation. Similarly, a word processor's spell-checker will catch misspelled words in a requirements specification, but it cannot spot erroneous, ambiguous, or missing requirements or incorrect word usage.

Testing doesn't tell you anything about the clarity or maintainability of the code, but a developer can judge these qualities during a review. A human reviewer can spot unclear error messages, inadequate comments, hard-coded variable values, and repeated code patterns that could be consolidated. Testing won't reveal unnecessary code, although code analyzers can flag unreachable code that a person might not notice. You could use a test coverage analyzer to identify untested code, such as exception handlers that are hard to trigger, and then focus your manual review on those code segments.

A student in a seminar once protested that peer reviews were unnecessary, insisting that she could find all the errors faster by testing. This is a common misconception. IBM's Santa Teresa laboratory found that, on average, 3.5 labor hours were needed to find a major defect by code inspection versus 15 to 25 hours of testing (Kaplan 1995). Within a single testing stage, you are unlikely to remove more than 35 percent of the errors in the tested work product. In contrast, design and code inspections typically remove between 50 and 70 percent of the defects present (C. Jones 1996). Highly experienced inspectors can attain 90 percent removal effectiveness. Unless you are using a code coverage analyzer to measure your unit testing, you're probably not testing more than 60 percent of your code (M. Johnson 1994). Without a coverage analyzer, you don't know what parts of the code your test suite didn't execute. However, you do know exactly what code you examined in a peer review.

A test might reveal a failure—an execution outcome in which the system does not exhibit the expected behavior—and then you have to go on a debugging expedition to find the underlying defect. During a review, however, you are looking directly at the problem, not at an indirect symptom of it. Reviews also expose defects that testing tools might be blocked from detecting. For example, if a button on a dialog box doesn't function properly, you have to fix it before you can test the display that's supposed to appear when the user clicks that button. However, you can review the code for that second display in spite of the button bug. Peer reviews are the best available tool for finding defects in requirements and design specifications, project plans, user manuals, and similar documents. And how else can you "test" your test plans, designs, and cases except through manual review?

In a multistep process such as software development, the quality of what comes out of any process step is limited by the quality of the inputs to that step. Figure 1–1 illustrates a typical sequence of activities involved in software development, showing major checkpoints at which reviews are necessary. This figure

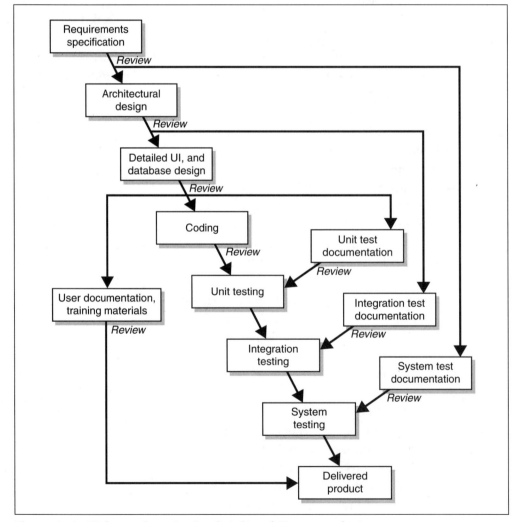

Figure 1–1. Major review checkpoints in a software project

resembles the oft-criticized waterfall life cycle, but it doesn't mean to imply that you must fully specify all the requirements before commencing design and complete the design before coding can begin. Many projects perform successive portions of each activity to build a product through a sequence of releases having increasing functionality. Regardless of the development life cycle you follow, a peer review provides an important quality gate through which each major deliverable should pass before you perform subsequent work based on that deliverable.

Do not expect to replace testing with peer reviews; rather, add reviews to your quality tool kit. Reviews can often improve product quality more cheaply than testing can, and they can reduce the cost and duration of testing. For example, one operating-system development organization reported that finding a design defect in testing required an average of 8.5 labor hours, compared to just 1.4 labor hours through inspection (Ackerman, Buchwald, and Lewski 1989). Combining reviews with static and dynamic code analyzers, dynamic testing, test coverage tools, and interactive debuggers provides powerful defect-detection capabilities.

What Can Be Reviewed

Although many people associate peer reviews with code, virtually any software engineering or project management work product can benefit from peer review. The Institute of Electrical and Electronics Engineers' "Standard for Software Reviews" (Std 1028-1997) lists 37 types of software-related work products that are candidates for review (IEEE 1999b). Here are some deliverables to consider reviewing:

- Marketing documents, requirements specifications, use cases, and analysis models
- Business process models and business rules
- Project charter documents and all kinds of project plans (project management plan, task list, schedule, configuration management plan, quality assurance plan, risk management plan, and so on)
- Architecture descriptions
- User interface designs and prototypes (Nielsen and Mack 1994; Constantine and Lockwood 1999)
- Software and database design descriptions and models
- Source code, including scripts, macros, stored procedures, and the like
- Program documentation and system maintenance documentation

- Test plans, designs, cases, and procedures
- User guides, reference manuals, help screens, tutorials, training materials, and field and customer support manuals
- Build, release, and installation procedures
- Software development procedures, standards, and process descriptions

Even though this book is titled *Peer Reviews in Software,* the same review methods can be applied to non-software engineering work products. They also work for nontechnical documents in which correctness, continuity, and consistency are essential.

Because of the defect-repair cost amplification, the highest leverage comes from reviewing early-stage project deliverables. One division at a multinational imaging company measured an ROI of ten to one from inspecting requirements specifications over a period of five years. At Lockheed Martin Western Development Labs, inspections of requirements documents discovered more defects per hour than did design or code inspections (Bourgeois 1996). Because requirements provide the foundation for all the other work done on a project, formal inspection of all requirements documents is perhaps the most important software quality practice.

A Personal Commitment to Quality

A sign on the wall of my high school chemistry class asked, "If you don't have time to do it right, when will you have time to do it over?" People in the software industry should take this message to heart. If you don't have time to use peer reviews to improve your product quality, you'll need even more time to fix the defects that your testers and customers find. Use your accumulated review experiences to enhance your development processes so your team members make fewer errors in their work, thereby saving even more time.

As we'll explore in Chapter 2, how well peer reviews will work for your team depends on the team's culture and the attitudes of your team members. If you're serious about the quality of your personal work, you'll accept that you make mistakes, seek the counsel of your compatriots in finding them, and willingly review your colleagues' work products. You will set aside your ego so that you can benefit from the experience and perspective of your technical peers. When you have internalized the benefits of peer reviews, you won't feel comfortable unless someone else carefully examines any significant deliverable you create.

CHAPTER TWO

A Little Help from Your Friends

Asking other people to point out errors in your work is a learned—not instinctive—behavior. We all take pride in the work we do. We don't like to admit we make mistakes, we don't realize how many we make (or we would correct them ourselves), and we don't like to ask someone else to find them. If you're going to hold successful peer reviews, you have to overcome this natural resistance to outside critique of your work.

Peer reviews are as much a social interaction as a technical practice. Instilling a review program into an organization requires an understanding of that organization's culture and the values its members hold. Managers need to believe that the time spent on reviews is a sound business investment so they will make time available for the team to hold reviews. You need to understand why certain people resist submitting their work to scrutiny by their colleagues and address that resistance. You also must educate the team and its managers about the peer review process, appropriate behavior during reviews, and the benefits that getting a little help from their friends can provide both to individuals and to the organization.

Scratch Each Other's Backs

Busy practitioners are sometimes reluctant to spend time examining a colleague's work. You might be leery of a co-worker who asks you to review his code. Does he lack confidence? Does he want you to do his thinking for him?

"Anyone who needs his code reviewed shouldn't be getting paid as a software developer," scoff some review resisters.

In a healthy software engineering culture, team members engage their peers to improve the quality of their work and increase their productivity. They understand that the time they spend looking at a colleague's work product is repaid when other team members examine their own deliverables. The best software engineers I have known actively sought out reviewers. Indeed, the input from many reviewers over their careers was part of what made these developers the best.

Gerald Weinberg introduced the concept of "egoless programming" in 1971 in *The Psychology of Computer Programming,* which was reissued in 1998 (Weinberg 1998). Egoless programming addresses the fact that people tie much of their perception of self-worth to their work. You can interpret a fault someone finds in an item you created as a shortcoming in yourself as a software developer—and perhaps even as a human being. To guard your ego, you don't want to know about all the errors you've made. Your ego might be so protective that you deny the possibility that you made errors and attempt to rationalize possible bugs into features.

Such staunch ego-protection presents a barrier to effective peer review, leads to an attitude of private ownership of an individual's contributions to a team project, and can result in a poor-quality product. Egoless programming enables an author to step back and let others point out places where improvement is needed in a product he created. Practitioners of egoless programming also understand that their products should be easy for others to understand. In contrast, some programmers enjoy writing obscure, clever code that only they can understand, with the notion that this makes them somehow superior to others who struggle to comprehend it. A manager who values egoless programming will encourage a culture of collaborative teamwork, shared rewards for success, and the open exchange of knowledge among team members.

Note that the term is "egoless programming," not "egoless programmer." People are entitled to protect their egos. Developers need a robust enough ego to trust and defend their work, but not so much ego that they reject suggestions for better solutions. Software professionals take pride in the things they create. However, they also recognize that people make mistakes and can benefit from outside perspectives. The egoless reviewer has compassion and sensitivity for his colleagues, if for no reason other than that their roles will be reversed one day.

Reviews and Team Culture

While individual participants can always benefit from a peer review, a broad review program can succeed only in a culture that values quality. "Quality" has many dimensions, including freedom from defects, satisfaction of customer needs, timeliness of delivery, and the possession of desirable product functionality and attributes. Members of a software engineering culture regard reviews as constructive activities that help both individuals and teams succeed. They understand that reviews are not intended to identify inferior performers or to find scapegoats for quality problems.

Reviews can result in two undesirable attitudes on the part of the work product's author. Some people become lax in their work because they're relying on someone else to find their mistakes, just as some programmers expect testers to catch their errors. The author is ultimately responsible for the product; a review is just an aid to help the author create a high-quality deliverable. Sometimes when I'm reading a draft of an article or book chapter I've written, I hear a little voice telling me that a section is incorrect or awkwardly phrased. I used to tell myself, "I'll give it to the reviewers and see what they think." Big mistake: the reviewers invariably disliked that clumsy section. Now whenever I hear that little voice, I fix the problem before I waste my reviewers' time.

The other extreme to avoid is the temptation to perfect the product before you allow another pair of eyes to see it. This is an ego-protecting strategy: you won't feel embarrassed about your mistakes if no one else sees them. I once managed a developer who refused to let anyone review her code until it was complete and as good as she could make it—fully implemented, tested, formatted, and documented. She regarded a review as a seal of approval rather than as the in-process quality-improvement activity it really is.

Such reluctance has several unfortunate consequences. If your work isn't reviewed until you think it's complete, you are psychologically resistant to suggestions for changes. If the program runs, how bad can it be? You are likely to rationalize away possible bugs because you believe you've finished and you're eager to move on to the next task. Relying on your own deskchecking and unit testing ignores the greater efficiency of a peer review for finding many defects.

At the same time, the desire to show our colleagues only our best side can become a positive factor. Reviews motivate us to practice superior craftsmanship because we know our coworkers will closely examine our work. In this indirect way, peer reviews lead to higher quality. One of my fellow consultants knows a quality engineer who began to present his team with summaries of defects found during reviews, without identifying specific work products or authors. The team soon saw a decrease in the number of bugs discovered during reviews. Based on what he knew about the team, my colleague concluded that authors created better products after they learned how reviews were being used on the project and knew what kinds of defects to look for. Reviews weren't a form of punishment but stimulated a desire to complete a body of work properly.

The Influence of Culture

In a healthy software engineering culture, a set of shared beliefs, individual behaviors, and technical practices define an environment in which all team members are committed to building quality products through the effective application of sensible processes (Wiegers 1996a). Such a culture demands a commitment by managers at all levels to provide a quality-driven environment. Recognizing that team success depends on helping each other do the best possible job, members of a healthy culture prefer to have peers, not customers, find software defects. Having a coworker locate a defect is regarded as a "good catch," not as a personal failing.

Peer reviews have their greatest impact in a healthy software culture, and a successful review program contributes strongly to creating such a culture. Prerequisites for establishing and sustaining an effective review program include:

- Defining and communicating your business goals for each project so reviewers can refer to a shared project vision
- Determining your customers' expectations for product quality so you can set attainable quality goals
- Understanding how peer reviews and other quality practices can help the team achieve its quality goals
- Educating stakeholders within the development organization—and, where appropriate, in the customer community—about what peer reviews are, why they add value, who should participate, and how to perform them
- Providing the necessary staff time to define and manage the organization's review process, train the participants, conduct the reviews, and collect and evaluate review data

The dynamics between the work product's author and its reviewers are critical. The author must trust and respect the reviewers enough to be receptive to their comments. Similarly, the reviewers must show respect for the author's talent and hard work. Reviewers should thoughtfully select the words they use to raise an issue, focusing on what they observed about the product. Saying, "I didn't see where these variables were initialized" is likely to elicit a constructive response, whereas "You didn't initialize these variables" might get the author's hackles up. The small shift in wording from the accusatory "you" to the less confrontational "I" lets the reviewer deliver even critical feedback effectively. Reviewers and authors must continue to work together outside the reviews, so they all need to maintain a level of professionalism and mutual respect to avoid strained relationships.

An author who walks out of a review meeting feeling embarrassed, personally attacked, or professionally insulted will not voluntarily submit work for peer review again. Nor do you want reviews to create authors who look forward to retaliating against their tormentors. The bad guys in a review are the bugs, not the author or the reviewers, but it takes several positive experiences to internalize this reality. The leaders of the review initiative should strive to create a culture of constructive criticism in which team members seek to learn from their peers and to do a better job the next time. To accelerate this culture change, managers should encourage and reward those who initially participate in reviews, regardless of the review outcomes.

Reviews and Managers

The attitude and behavior that managers exhibit toward reviews affect how well the reviews will work in an organization. Although managers want to deliver quality products, they also feel pressure to release products quickly. They don't always understand what peer reviews or inspections are or the contribution they make to shipping quality products on time. I once encountered resistance to inspections from a quality manager who came from a manufacturing background. He regarded inspections as a carryover from the old manufacturing quality practice of manually examining finished products for defects. After he understood how software inspections contribute to quality through early removal of defects, his resistance disappeared.

Managers need to learn about peer reviews and their impact on the organization so they can build the reviews into project plans, allocate resources for them, and communicate their commitment to reviews to the team. If reviews aren't planned, they won't happen. Managers also must be sensitive to the interpersonal aspects of peer reviews. Watch out for known culture killers, such as managers singling out certain developers for the humiliating "punishment" of having their work reviewed.

Without visible and sustained commitment to peer reviews from management, only those practitioners who believe reviews are important will perform them. Management commitment to any engineering practice is more than providing verbal support or giving team members permission to use the practice. Figure 2–1 lists eleven signs of management commitment to peer reviews.

To persuade managers about the value of reviews, couch your argument in terms of what outcomes are important to the manager's view of success. Published data convinces some people, but others want to see tangible benefits from a pilot or trial application in their own organization. Still other managers will reject both logical and data-based arguments for reviews and simply say no. In this case, keep in mind one of my basic software engineering cultural principles—"Never let your boss or your customer talk you into doing a bad job"—and engage your colleagues in reviews anyway (perhaps quietly, to avoid unduly provoking your managers).

A dangerous situation arises when a manager wishes to use data collected from peer reviews to assess the performance of the authors (Lee 1997). Software

---

Eleven Signs of Management Commitment to Peer Reviews

1. Providing the resources and time to develop, implement, and sustain an effective review process
2. Setting policies, expectations, and goals about review practice
3. Maintaining the practice of reviews even when projects are under time pressure
4. Ensuring that project schedules include time for reviews
5. Making training available to the participants and attending the training themselves
6. Never using review results to evaluate the performance of individuals
7. Holding people accountable for participating in reviews and for contributing constructively to them
8. Publicly rewarding the early adopters of reviews to reinforce desired behaviors
9. Running interference with other managers and customers who challenge the need for reviews
10. Respecting the review team's appraisal of a document's quality
11. Asking for status reports on how the program is working, what it costs, and the team's benefits from reviews

Figure 2–1. Eleven signs of management commitment to peer reviews

metrics must *never* be used to reward or penalize individuals. The purposes of collecting data from reviews is to better understand your development and quality processes, to improve processes that aren't working well, and to track the impact of process changes. Using defect data from inspections to evaluate individuals is a classic culture killer. It can lead to *measurement dysfunction,* in which measurement motivates people to behave in a way that produces results inconsistent with the desired goals (Austin 1996).

I recently heard from a quality manager at a company that had operated a successful inspection program for two years. The development manager had just announced his intention to use inspection data as input to the performance evaluations of the work product authors. Finding more than five bugs during an inspection would count against the author. Naturally, this made the development team members very nervous. It conveyed the erroneous impression that the purpose of inspections is to punish people for making mistakes or to find someone to blame for troubled projects. This misapplication of inspection data could lead to numerous dysfunctional outcomes, including the following:

1. To avoid being punished for their results, developers might not submit their work for inspection. They might refuse to inspect a peer's work to avoid contributing to someone else's punishment.
2. Inspectors might not point out defects during the inspection, instead telling the author about them offline so they aren't tallied against the author. Alternatively, developers might hold "pre-reviews" to filter out bugs unofficially before going through a punitive inspection. This undermines the open focus on quality that should characterize inspection. It also skews any metrics you're legitimately tracking from multiple inspections.
3. Inspection teams might debate whether something really is a defect, because defects count against the author, and issues or simple questions do not. This could lead to glossing over actual defects.
4. The team's inspection culture might develop an implicit goal of finding few defects rather than revealing as many as possible. This reduces the value of the inspections without reducing their cost, thereby lowering the team's return on investment from inspections.
5. Authors might hold many inspections of small pieces of work to reduce the chance of finding more than five bugs in any one inspection. This leads to inefficient and time-wasting inspections. It's a kind of gamesmanship, doing the minimum to claim you have had your work inspected but not properly exploiting the technique.

These potential problems underscore the risks posed to an inspection program by using inspection data to evaluate individuals. Such evaluation criminalizes the mistakes we all make and pits team members against each other. It motivates participants to manipulate the process to avoid being hurt by it. If I were a developer in this situation, I would encourage management to have the organization's peer review coordinator (see Chapter 10) summarize defects collected from multiple inspections so the defect counts aren't linked to specific authors. If management insisted on using defect counts for performance appraisal, I would refuse to participate in inspections. Managers may legitimately expect developers to submit their work for review and to review deliverables that others create. However, a good manager doesn't need defect counts to know who the top contributors are and who is struggling.

When inspection metrics were introduced into one organization, a manager happily exclaimed, "This data will help me measure the performance of my engineers!" After the inspection champion explained the philosophy of software measurement to him, the manager agreed not to see the data from individual inspections. He publicly described the inspection process as a tool to help engineers produce better products. He told the engineers he would not view the individual inspection measures because he was interested in the big picture, the overall efficiency of the software engineering process. This manager's thoughtful comments helped defuse resistance to inspection measurement in his organization.

Why People Don't Do Reviews

If peer reviews are so great, why isn't everybody already doing them? Factors that contribute to the underuse of reviews include lack of knowledge about reviews, cultural issues, and simple resistance to change, often masquerading as excuses. If reviews aren't a part of your organization's standard practices, understand why so you know what must change to make them succeed.

Many people don't understand what peer reviews are, why they are valuable, the differences between informal reviews and inspections, or when and how to perform reviews. Education can solve this problem. Some developers and project managers don't think their projects are large enough or critical enough to need reviews. However, any body of work can benefit from an outside perspective.

The misperception that testing is always superior to manual examination also leads some practitioners to shun reviews. Testing has long been recognized as a critical activity in developing software. Entire departments are dedicated to testing, with testing effort scheduled into projects and resources allocated for testing. Organizations that have not yet internalized the benefits of peer reviews lack an analogous cultural imperative and a supporting infrastructure for performing them.

A fundamental cultural inhibitor to peer reviews is that developers don't recognize how many errors they make, so they don't see the need for methods to catch or reduce their errors. Many organizations don't collect, summarize, and present to all team members even such basic quality data as the number of errors found in testing or by customers. Authors who submit their work for scrutiny might feel that their privacy is being invaded, that they're being forced to air the internals of their work for all to see. This is threatening to some people, which is why the culture must emphasize the value of reviews as a collaborative, nonjudgmental tool for improved quality and productivity.

Previous unpleasant review experiences are a powerful cultural deterrent. The fear of management retribution or public ridicule if defects are discovered can make authors reluctant to let others examine their work. In poorly conducted reviews, authors can feel as though they—not their work—are being criticized, especially if personality conflicts already exist between specific individuals. Another cultural barrier is the attitude that the author is the most qualified person to examine his part of the system ("Who are you to look for errors in my work?"). Similarly, a common reaction from new developers who are invited to review the work of an experienced and respected colleague is, "Who am I to look for errors in his work?"

Traditional mechanisms for adopting improved practices are having practitioners observe what experienced role models do and having supervisors observe and coach new employees. In many software groups, though, each developer's methods remain private, and they don't have to change the way they work unless they wish to (Humphrey 2001). Paradoxically, many developers are reluctant to try a new method unless it has been proven to work, yet they don't believe the new approach works until they have successfully done it themselves. They don't want to take anyone else's word for it.

And then there are the excuses. Resistance often appears as NAH (not applicable here) syndrome (Jalote 2000). People who don't want to do reviews will expend considerable energy trying to explain why reviews don't fit their culture, needs, or time constraints. One excuse is the arrogant attitude that some people's work does not need reviewing. Some team members can't be bothered to look at a colleague's work. "I'm too busy fixing my own bugs to waste time finding someone else's." "Aren't we all supposed to be doing our own work correctly?" "It's not my problem if Jack has bugs in his code." Other developers imagine that their software prowess has moved them beyond needing peer reviews. "Inspections have been around for 25 years; they're obsolete. Our high-tech group uses only leading-edge technologies."

Protesting that the inspection process is too rigid for a go-with-the-flow development approach signals resistance to a practice that is perceived to add bureaucratic overhead. Indeed, the mere existence of a go-with-the-flow development process implies that long-term quality isn't a priority for the organization. Such a culture might have difficulty adopting formal peer reviews, although informal reviews might be palatable.

Overcoming Resistance to Reviews

To establish a successful review program, you must address existing barriers in the categories of knowledge, culture, and resistance to change. Lack of knowledge is easy to correct if people are willing to learn. My colleague Corinne found that the most vehement protesters in her organization were already doing informal reviews. They just didn't realize that a peer deskcheck is one type of peer review (see Chapter 3). Corinne discussed the benefits of formalizing some of these informal reviews and trying some inspections. A one-day class that includes a practice inspection gives team members a common understanding about peer reviews. Managers who also attend the class send powerful signals about their commitment to reviews. Management attendance says to the team, "This is important enough for me to spend time on it, so it should be important to you, too" and "I want to understand reviews so I can help make this effort succeed."

Dealing with cultural issues requires you to understand your team's culture and how best to steer the team members toward improved software engineering practices (Bouldin 1989; Caputo 1998; Weinberg 1997; Wiegers 1996a). What values do they hold in common? Do they share an understanding of—and a commitment to—quality? What previous change initiatives have succeeded and why? Which have struggled and why? Who are the opinion leaders in the group and what are their attitudes toward reviews?

Larry Constantine described four cultural paradigms found in software organizations: *closed, open, synchronous,* and *random* (Constantine 1993). A closed culture has a traditional hierarchy of authority. You can introduce peer reviews in a closed culture through a management-driven process improvement program, perhaps based on one of the Software Engineering Institute's capability maturity models. A management decree that projects will conduct reviews might succeed in a closed culture, but not in other types of organizations.

Innovation, collaboration, and consensus decision-making characterize an open culture. Members of an open culture want to debate the merits of peer reviews and participate in deciding when and how to implement them. Respected leaders who have had positive results with reviews in the past can influence the group's willingness to adopt them. Such cultures might prefer review meetings that include discussions of proposed solutions rather than inspections, which emphasize finding—not fixing—defects during meetings.

Members of a synchronous group are well aligned and comfortable with the status quo. Because they recognize the value of coordinating their efforts, they are probably already performing at least informal reviews. A comfort level with informal reviews eases implementation of an inspection program.

Entrepreneurial, fast-growing, and leading-edge companies often develop a random culture populated by autonomous individuals who like to go their own ways. In random organizations, individuals who have performed peer reviews in the past might continue to hold them. The other team members might not have the patience for reviews, although they could change their minds if quality problems from chaotic projects burn them badly enough.

However you describe your culture, people will want to know what benefits a new process will provide to them personally. A better way to react to a proposed process change is to ask, "What's in it for *us?*" Sometimes when you're asked to change the way you work, your immediate personal reward is small, although the team as a whole might benefit in a big way. I might not get three hours of benefit from spending three hours reviewing someone else's code. However, the other developer might avoid ten hours of debugging effort later in the project, and we might ship the product sooner than we would have otherwise.

Table 2–1 identifies some benefits various project team members might reap from reviewing major life-cycle deliverables. Of course, the customers also come out ahead. They receive a timely product that is more robust and reliable, better meets their needs, and increases their productivity. Higher customer satisfaction leads to business rewards all around.

Arrogant developers who believe reviews are beneath them might enjoy getting praise and respect from coworkers as they display their superior work during reviews. If influential resisters come to appreciate the value of peer reviews, they might persuade other team members to try them, too. A quality

Table 2–1. Benefits from Peer Reviews for Project Roles

Project Role	Possible Benefits from Peer Reviews
Developer	• Less time spent performing rework • Increased programming productivity • Confidence that the right requirements are being implemented • Better techniques learned from other developers • Reduced unit testing and debugging time • Less debugging during integration and system testing • Exchanging of information about components and the overall system with other team members
Development Manager	• Shortened product development cycle time • Reduced field service and customer support costs • Reduced lifetime maintenance costs, freeing resources for new development projects • Improved teamwork, collaboration, and development effectiveness • Better and earlier insight into project risks and quality issues
Maintainer	• Fewer production support demands, leading to a reduced maintenance backlog • More robust designs that tolerate change • Conformance of work products to team standards • More maintainable and better documented work products that are easy to understand and modify • Better understanding of the product from having participated in design and code reviews during development
Project Manager	• Increased likelihood that product will ship on schedule • Earlier visibility of quality issues • Reduced impact from staff turnover through cross-training of team members
Quality Assurance Manager	• Ability to judge the testability of product features under development • Shortened system-testing cycles and less retesting • Ability to use review data when making release decisions • Education of quality engineers about the product • Ability to anticipate quality assurance effort needed

continued

Table 2–1. Benefits from Peer Reviews for Project Roles (*cont.*)

Project Role	*Possible Benefits from Peer Reviews*
Requirements Analyst	• Earlier correction of missing or erroneous requirements • Fewer infeasible and untestable requirements because of developer and test engineer input during reviews
Test Engineer	• Ability to focus on finding subtle defects because product is of higher initial quality • Fewer defects that block continued testing • Improved test design and test cases that smooth out the testing process

manager once encountered a developer named Judy who was opposed to "time-sapping" inspections. After participating under protest, Judy quickly saw the power of the technique and became the group's leading convert. Because Judy had some influence with her peers, she helped turn developer resistance toward inspections into acceptance. Judy's project team ultimately asked the quality manager to help them hold even *more* inspections. Engaging developers in an effective inspection program helped motivate them to try some other software quality practices, too.

In another case, a newly hired system architect who had experienced the benefits of inspections in his previous organization was able to overcome resistance from members of his new team. The data this group collected from their inspections backed up the architect's conviction that they were well worth doing.

Peer Review Sophistication Scale

Figure 2–2 depicts a scale of an organization's sophistication in its practice of software peer reviews (for a similar scale, see Grady 1997). The value added to the organization is greater at the higher stages. Use this scale to calibrate your organization's current review performance and see what it would take to enhance it.

In the worst case (stage 0), no one in the organization performs reviews. Stage 1 is a small advance, with team members holding impromptu "over-the-shoulder" reviews. Perhaps the team members haven't heard about peer reviews or don't think they have time to do them. They might have rejected reviews as inappropriate for their project for some reason.

At stage 2, team members periodically hold unstructured reviews. The participants might not realize there are different types of peer reviews. They have not adopted a common review vocabulary or process. They might hold a walk-through or other informal review and call it an inspection, even though it did not conform to an actual inspection process. The team's review objectives include both finding defects and exchanging knowledge.

By stage 3, the project team holds reviews routinely. They are built into the project schedule and the team understands how to perform structured, formal reviews such as inspections. The organization has adopted a peer review process that incorporates multiple review methods, using standard forms and defect

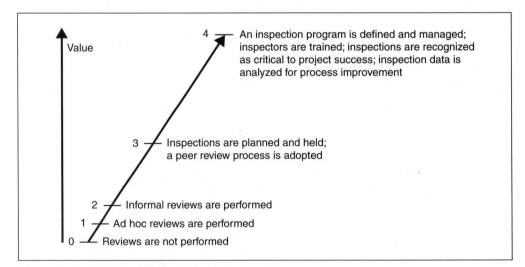

Figure 2–2. Peer review sophistication scale

checklists. You don't need to start at the bottom of the scale, so aim to begin at least at stage 3, incorporating inspections into routine practice. This will keep you from getting stuck at a lower level and missing out on the full benefits of formal peer reviews.

The most successful organizations reach stage 4, which represents a paradigm shift to a new way for the organization to create software products. Stage 4 organizations have established an official inspection program, staffed with a peer review coordinator and managed by a peer review process owner (see Chapter 10). They have identified the various kinds of work products that will be inspected. All participants and managers are trained in inspection. The review coordinator verifies that inspections are conducted as scheduled and collects data from them. These data are analyzed for product quality assessment, process improvement, and defect prevention. Inspections are recognized as critical contributors to project success, and the team members would not be comfortable working in an environment where peer review was not a standard practice.

Planning for Reviews

If you don't plan reviews as project tasks and allocate resources to them, they can appear to slow the project down, as does any unanticipated work. Your team can hold informal, ad hoc reviews whenever someone desires constructive input from coworkers. However, frequent unplanned reviews will drain time from the reviewers, who might be less likely to request or participate in these informal reviews.

Incorporate formal reviews into the project's schedule or work breakdown structure. A well-defined software development life cycle itemizes specific exit criteria for key phase deliverables, including passing an appropriate peer review. Figure 1–1 illustrated the major project checkpoints at which you should schedule reviews. Some teams use planning checklists of the tasks required for common project activities, such as implementing a module or an object class. Include reviews on such checklists. Also conduct interim reviews of major deliverables prior to completion to ensure they are meeting their quality goals. Informal reviews can let you judge whether a deliverable is ready for inspection and can serve as quick quality filters from an outside viewpoint.

The effort you devote to peer reviews might seem like extra overhead, but it is not really additional time in your project schedule. Think of it as a reallocation of effort you would otherwise spend on testing and the pervasive rework of debugging, patching in missed requirements, and so on. Keeping records of reviews and their benefits will help you judge the appropriate level of investment needed to meet your project's quality goals.

Project planners sometimes treat reviews as milestones, as shown in Figure 2–3. However, in project-planning terms, a milestone is a state, not an activity. Milestones have a duration of zero time and consume no resources, so treating reviews as tasks in your plan, as Figure 2–4 illustrates, is more accurate. The milestone is reached when you deem that the deliverable has passed the review. If you treat reviews as milestones, the project schedule can appear to slip when you perform reviews, because the effort they require was not anticipated. Depending on the kind of reviews you hold, review tasks will include effort for individual preparation, review meetings, or both. You should also plan to perform rework after every quality control activity, but your team will spend less time on rework as its development practices improve.

How can you estimate how much time to plan for preparation, review meetings, and rework? If you keep even simple records of the time your team members actually spend on these activities, you can make better estimates for future

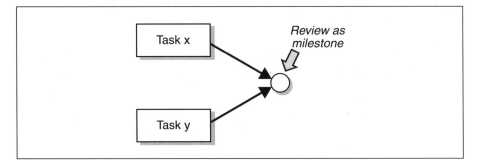

Figure 2–3. WRONG: Review treated as a milestone

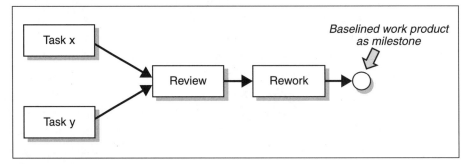

Figure 2–4. RIGHT: Review and rework treated as tasks

reviews. Data on the most effective rates of coverage of material during preparation and in review meetings will help you judge the time needed for these review stages (see Chapter 5). Without such data, you are never estimating—you're guessing.

Guiding Principles for Reviews

All peer reviews should follow several basic principles to make them powerful contributors to product quality and team culture (Wiegers 1996a). First, ***check your egos at the door.*** There are two aspects to being egoless. As an author, keep an open mind and be receptive to suggestions for improvements. Avoid the temptation to argue every point raised, defend your decisions to the death, or explain away errors. As a reviewer, remember that you're not trying to show how much smarter you are than the author.

Another useful guideline is to ***keep the review team small,*** generally between three and seven participants. Larger teams make the review more expensive without adding proportionate value. They slow the rate at which the group can cover material in a review meeting. Large groups are prone to distracting side conversations and can easily go off on time-wasting tangents. Chapter 12 suggests what to do if a lot of people wish to participate in a review.

The prime objective of a peer review is defect detection, so strive to ***find problems during reviews, but don't try to solve them.*** Technical people like to tackle challenging problems; that's why we're in the software business. However, the author should fix the identified problems *after* the review meeting, working with selected reviewers on specific issues to reap the benefits of another's experience. Formal reviews, such as inspections, include a moderator or review leader role. As described in Chapter 5, the inspection moderator is responsible for keeping the meeting focused on finding defects and for limiting problem-solving discussions to just a minute or two. If you don't use a moderator, the participants will have to monitor themselves so the meeting doesn't derail into an extended brainstorming session on the first bug found.

Another guiding principle is to ***limit review meetings to about two hours.*** My friend Matt once pointed out to me that "the mind cannot absorb what the body cannot endure." When you are distracted by physical discomfort or exhaustion, you're no longer an effective reviewer. Take a short break halfway through a long review meeting, and come back tomorrow to finish if you didn't properly cover all the material in the first meeting. Scope the work into logical chunks that the team can examine in one to two hours, based on your organization's historical rates for reviewing or inspecting different types of work products (see Chapter 5).

To use the team's time as efficiently as possible, ***require advance preparation*** for formal reviews. During informal review meetings, participants come in cold and listen to the author describe his work. Serious defect-hunting efforts, such as inspection, demand that the meeting participants have already examined the product on their own to understand it and find issues to raise during the meeting. The participants need to receive the review materials several days prior to the meeting to give them time to prepare for the inspection meeting.

Being sensitive to the human and cultural issues of peer reviews and following these basic guidelines will maximize the contribution reviews make to your development and maintenance projects.

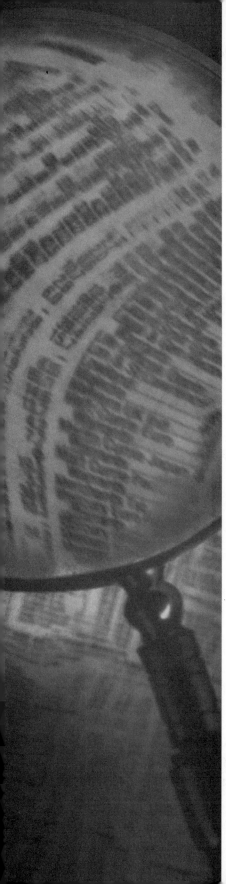

CHAPTER THREE

Peer Review Formality Spectrum

I have been using the terms "review" and "peer review" as synonyms meaning any manual examination performed to look for errors in a software deliverable. However, there are several distinct review approaches. The software literature contains conflicting definitions and inconsistent usage for the names of these activities. For example, "walkthrough" has been used to describe many types of reviews, ranging from casual group discussions to formal inspections. One organization changed its walkthrough process to an inspection process simply by globally replacing the word "walkthrough" with "inspection." It really was an inspection process, although the original authors had mistakenly used the walkthrough terminology.

This chapter describes several kinds of peer reviews that span a range of formality and rigor. It also suggests ways to select an appropriate review technique for a given situation. You might be accustomed to different terminology, but I'm presenting these descriptions here to provide a common vocabulary for this book.

The Formality Spectrum

Peer reviews can be classified based on their degree of formality or their relative levels of discipline and flexibility (Iisakka, Tervonen, and Harjumaa 1999). Figure 3–1 places several common review methods along a formality scale.

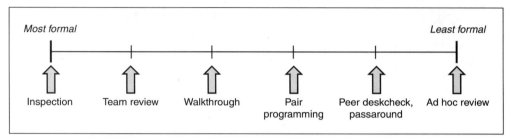

Figure 3–1. Peer review formality spectrum

These are not the only types of technical peer reviews, and multiple variations of many of them exist. The most formal reviews, such as inspections, have several characteristics:

- Defined objectives
- Participation by a trained team
- Leadership by a trained moderator
- Specific participant roles and responsibilities
- A documented review procedure
- Reporting of results to management
- Explicit entry and exit criteria
- Tracking of defects to closure
- Recording of process and quality data

Informal reviews may well meet your needs in certain situations. They are quick and cheap, do not require advance planning, demand no organizational infrastructure, and can help the author proceed on an improved course. Learn about the strengths and limitations of the various approaches so you can select a review process for each situation that fits your culture, time constraints, and business and technical objectives. I recommend that you begin performing inspections at the outset to gain experience so you can judge when a less formal review approach is appropriate and when it is not. If you start by holding just informal reviews with the intention of moving to inspections someday, you'll miss out on the full advantages of inspection.

All peer reviews involve some combination of planning, individual examination of the work product, review meetings, correction of errors, and verification of the corrections. Table 3–1 shows which of these activities are typically included in each of the review types shown in Figure 3–1.

Table 3–1. Activities Typically Included in Different Types of Peer Reviews

Review Type	Activity				
	Planning	Preparation	Meeting	Correction	Verification
Inspection	Yes	Yes	Yes	Yes	Yes
Team Review	Yes	Yes	Yes	Yes	No
Walkthrough	Yes	No	Yes	Yes	No
Pair Programming	Yes	No	Continuous	Yes	Yes
Peer Deskcheck, Passaround	No	Yes	Possibly	Yes	No
Ad Hoc Review	No	No	Yes	Yes	No

Inspection

An *inspection* is the most systematic and rigorous type of peer review (Ebenau and Strauss 1994; Fagan 1976; Gilb and Graham 1993; Radice 2001). The term "formal inspection" is redundant but is sometimes used for emphasis. Inspection has been identified as a software industry best practice, while less formal review approaches have not earned this status (Boehm and Basili 2001; Brown 1996; McConnell 1996). Inspection follows a multistage process with specific roles assigned to individual participants. Although several variations on the inspection theme have been developed, their similarities outweigh their differences. Chapter 4 describes a common inspection process that includes seven stages: planning, overview, preparation, meeting, rework, follow-up, and causal analysis.

For maximum effectiveness, inspectors should be trained in the inspection process so they can perform the various participant roles. Inspections rely on checklists of defects commonly found in different types of software work products and other analytical techniques to search for bugs. Some reasons to hold inspections include the following (IEEE 1999b):

- To verify that a product satisfies its functional specifications, specified quality attributes, and customer needs and to identify any deviations from these
- To verify that a product conforms to pertinent standards, regulations, rules, plans, and procedures and to identify any deviations from these

- To provide metrics on defects and inspection effort that can lead to improvements in both the inspection process and the organization's software engineering process (see Chapter 9)

An important aspect of an inspection is that participants other than the work product's author lead the meeting (inspection role of *moderator*), present the material to the inspection team (*reader*), and document issues as they are brought up (*recorder*) (IEEE 1999b). Compared to other reviews, inspection provides the most thorough coverage of the work products. The participants prepare for the inspection meeting by examining the material on their own. During the meeting, the reader presents one small portion of the material at a time to the other inspectors, who then raise issues, ask questions, and point out possible defects. Because several inspectors carefully scrutinize the product, inspection provides a good test of understandability and maintainability. The use of a reader helps the team members reach the same interpretation of each portion of the product, because the inspectors can compare their understanding to that expressed by the reader. At the end of the inspection meeting, the team agrees on an appraisal of the work product and judges whether changes the author will make during rework must be verified through a second inspection, by a single person, or not at all.

Inspections are more effective at finding defects than are informal reviews. One telecommunications company detected an average of 16 to 20 defects per thousand lines of code by inspection, compared to only three defects per thousand lines of code when using informal reviews. Inspections are especially important for high-risk products that must be as free of defects as possible. The close scrutiny of an inspection helps reveal programming problems such as off-by-one errors, incorrect arguments in function calls, missing cases, and situations in which one routine will cause problems in another.

Different inspectors spot different kinds of problems, but this contribution does not increase linearly with additional participants. Many defects are found redundantly. When one inspector notes a defect, it's common to hear another participant say, "I saw that, too." The interactions between inspectors during the meeting can reveal new problems as one person's observation stimulates another's thinking. Michael Fagan, who developed the best-known inspection method, termed this synergy the Phantom Inspector (Fagan 1986). Although some studies have questioned whether synergy adds significant value, a peer review that does not include a meeting loses this potential collaborative benefit.

Team Review

Team reviews are a type of "inspection-lite," being planned and structured but less formal and less rigorous than inspections. A team review allows a group of qualified people to judge whether a product is suitable for use and to identify ways in which the product does not satisfy its specifications. The team review goes by many names, often simply being called a "review." The structured walk-through approach devised by Edward Yourdon is similar to what I term a team review (Yourdon 1989). Team reviews cost more than having a single colleague perform a peer deskcheck, but the different participants will find different problems. A team review provides a good learning opportunity for the participants.

As I have practiced them, team reviews follow several of the steps found in an inspection. The participants receive the review materials several days prior to the review meeting and are expected to study the materials on their own. The team collects data on the review effort and the defects found. The overview and follow-up inspection stages are simplified or omitted, however, and some participant roles may be combined. As with any meeting, the team can get sidetracked on tangential discussions, so a moderator is needed to keep the meeting on course. A recorder or scribe captures issues as they are raised during the discussion, using standard forms the organization has adopted.

The guidelines and procedures for inspection described in this book also apply to team reviews except in the way the review meeting is conducted. The author might lead a team review, whereas in an inspection the author is not permitted to serve as the moderator. In contrast to most inspections, the reader role is omitted. Instead of having one participant describe a small chunk of the product at a time, the moderator asks the participants if they have any issues on a specific section or page.

Although little published data is available, one industry study found that this type of team review discovered only two-thirds as many defects per hour as inspections revealed (Van Veenendaal 1999). IBM Federal Systems Division measured coding productivity for projects that practiced structured walkthroughs (team reviews) at about half the productivity of similar projects that used inspections (Gilb and Graham 1993). Team reviews are suitable for a group or work product that doesn't require the full rigor of the inspection process. Being less formal than inspection, team reviews might also devote some meeting time to discussing solution ideas and having participants reach consensus on technical approaches.

Walkthrough

A *walkthrough* is an informal review in which the author of a work product describes the product to a group of peers and solicits comments (Hollocker 1990). Walkthroughs differ significantly from inspections because the author takes the dominant role; other specific review roles are usually not defined. Whereas an inspection is intended to meet the team's quality objectives, a walkthrough principally serves the needs of the author. Table 3–2 points out some differences between the ways that inspections, team reviews, and walkthroughs (as I'm defining them here) usually are performed.

Walkthroughs are informal because they typically do not follow a defined procedure, do not specify exit criteria, require no management reporting, and generate no metrics (Fagan 1986). They can be an efficient way to examine work products modified during maintenance, because the author can draw the reviewers' attention to those portions of the deliverables that were changed. However, this runs the risk of overlooking other sections that should have been changed but were not. Because records are rarely kept, there is little data about how effec-

Table 3–2. Comparison of Some Inspection, Team Review, and Walkthrough Characteristics

Characteristic	Inspection	Team Review	Walkthrough
Leader	Moderator	Moderator or Author	Author
Material presenter	Reader	Moderator	Author
Granularity of material presented	Small chunks	Pages or sections	Author's discretion
Recorder used	Yes	Yes	Maybe
Documented procedure followed	Yes	Maybe	Maybe
Specific participant roles	Yes	Yes	No
Defect checklists used	Yes	Yes	No
Data collected and analyzed	Yes	Maybe	No
Product appraisal determined	Yes	Yes	No

tive walkthroughs are at detecting bugs. One report from Ford Motor Company indicated that inspections found 50 percent more defects per thousand lines of code than did walkthroughs (Bankes and Sauer 1995).

When walkthroughs do not follow a defined procedure, people perform them in diverse ways that range from casual to disciplined. In a typical walkthrough, the author presents a code module or design component to the participants, describing what it does in the product, how it is structured and how it performs its tasks, the logic flow, and its inputs and outputs. Finding problems is one goal. Another is reaching a shared understanding and agreement as to the module's purpose, structure, and implementation. Design walkthroughs provide a way to assess whether the proposed design is sufficiently robust and appropriate to solve the problem. Arguing the correctness and soundness of a proposed design leads to improvement as well as to defect detection.

Authors can use walkthroughs to test their ideas, brainstorm alternative solutions, and stimulate the creative aspects of the development process. Walkthroughs are a good way to evaluate test documentation. The author can lead the team through the test cases to reach a common understanding of how the system should behave under specified conditions. Usability walkthroughs are a tool for evaluating a user interface design from a human factors perspective (Bias 1991).

A walkthrough is appropriate when a prime review objective is to educate others about the product. You can include more people in a walkthrough than can participate effectively in an inspection. However, walkthroughs don't let the participants judge how understandable the product is on its own. After the walkthrough, you aren't sure if you understood the material because it was well structured or because the author presented it clearly (Freedman and Weinberg 1990).

If you don't fully understand some information presented in a walkthrough, you might gloss over it and assume the author is right. It's easy to be swayed into silence by an author's rationalization of his approach, even if you aren't convinced. Sometimes, though, a reviewer's confusion is a clue that a defect lurks nearby or that something needs to be expressed more clearly. My colleague Kevin once worked with a "technical expert" who created designs that no one else could understand during walkthroughs. At first, Kevin's group assumed this developer was wiser than they were. Eventually, though, they realized that he just created convoluted designs. They tried using formal inspections to rein him in. Unfortunately, their manager was fooled by the "expert's" apparent brilliance and let him continue to design and code in a vacuum. Reviews won't help people who reject all suggestions from their colleagues.

In the past, the programmer often stepped through a module's execution during a walkthrough, using some sample data, with his peers checking for correct logic and behavior. Interactive debuggers are more commonly used for this purpose today. Another walkthrough strategy involves following a script that describes a specific task or scenario to illustrate how the system would function during a sample user session. This technique helps a group of customers, requirements analysts, and developers reach agreement on the system's behavior. It can also reveal errors in early deliverables such as requirements specifications. Walkthroughs have a place in your peer review tool kit, but the domination by the author and the unstructured approach render them a less valuable defect filter than inspections or team reviews.

Pair Programming

Pair programming is a component of a popular "agile methodology" approach to software development called Extreme Programming (Beck 2000). In pair programming, two developers work on the same program simultaneously at a single workstation. This approach facilitates communication and permits continuous, incremental, and informal review of each person's ideas. Every line of code is written by two brains driving a single set of fingers, which leads to superior work products by literally applying the adage "two heads are better than one." The member of the pair who is currently doing the typing is the driver, while the other is the partner (Jeffries, Anderson, and Hendrickson 2001). The driver and partner exchange roles from time to time.

Culturally, pair programming promotes collaboration, an attitude of collective ownership of the team's code base, and a shared commitment to the quality of each component (Williams and Kessler 2000). Two team members become intimately familiar with every piece of code, which reduces the knowledge lost through staff turnover. The pair can quickly make course corrections because of the real-time review by the partner. Rapid iteration leads to robust designs and programs. The pair programming technique can be applied to create other software deliverables besides code.

I classify pair programming as a type of informal review because it is unstructured and involves no process, preparation, or documentation. It lacks the outside perspective of someone who is not personally attached to the code that a formal review brings. Nor does it include the author of the parent work product as a separate perspective. Pair programming is not specifically a review technique. Instead, it is a software development strategy that relies on the synergy of two focused minds to create products superior in design, execution, and quality.

Some evidence indicates that pair programming leads to higher product quality and accelerates completion of programs compared to the time needed by individuals (Williams et al. 2000). However, pair programming constitutes a major culture change in the way a development team operates, so it's not a simple replacement for traditional peer reviews in most situations.

Peer Deskcheck

In the early days of programming, we studied our source listings carefully between infrequent compilations to find errors in the hope of ensuring a clean execution. This is a *deskcheck*. Contemporary code editors and fast compilations greatly enhance developer productivity, but they have also made us less disciplined about reviewing our own work. Don't underestimate the value of careful deskchecks. Meticulously examining a printed listing reveals far more errors than you'll see by scanning the code on your monitor. Deskchecking is an integral aspect of the highly regarded Personal Software Process (Humphrey 1995). A deskcheck is a kind of self-review, not a peer review.

In a *peer deskcheck* (also known as a buddy check and pair reviewing), only one person besides the author examines the work product. The author might not know how the reviewer approached the task or how comprehensively the review was done. A peer deskcheck depends entirely on the single reviewer's knowledge, skill, and self-discipline, so expect wide variability in results. Peer deskchecks can be fairly formal if the reviewer employs defect checklists, specific analysis methods, and standard forms to keep records for the team's review metrics collection. Upon completion, the reviewer can deliver a defect list to the author, they can sit down together to prepare the defect list, or the reviewer can simply hand the author the marked-up work product.

The peer deskcheck is the cheapest review approach. It involves only one reviewer's time, which might include a follow-up discussion with the author to explain the reviewer's findings. This method is suitable if you have colleagues who are skilled at finding defects on their own, if you have severe time and resource restrictions, or for low-risk work products. A peer deskcheck can be more comfortable for the author than a group review; however, the errors found will only be those the one reviewer is best at spotting. Also, the author is not present to answer questions and hear discussions that can help him find additional defects no one else sees. You can address this shortcoming by having the author and the single reviewer sit down together in what has been termed a two-person inspection (Bisant and Lyle 1989). The two-person inspection lacks a moderator, and the one inspector also functions as the reader.

Peer deskchecks provide a good way to begin developing a review culture. Find a colleague you respect professionally and trust personally and offer to exchange work products for peer deskchecks. This is also a good mentoring method, providing it's done with sensitivity. Senior developers at Microsoft review code written by new people or by developers working in a new area (Cusumano and Selby 1995). In addition to providing a quality filter, such reviews provide a coaching opportunity to pass along tips for better ways to do things the next time. Be careful, though: there is a thin line between asking an old hand to help out a junior developer and implying that incompetent programmers need someone to second-guess their work.

Passaround

A *passaround* or distribution is a multiple, concurrent peer deskcheck. Instead of asking just one colleague for input, the author delivers a copy of the product to several people and collates their feedback. This book was reviewed by using a passaround approach, with an average of about 16 people providing comments on each chapter. Some comments were superficial, while others led to significant restructuring and major improvement. As is common with a passaround, I never heard from several people who volunteered to participate, and others returned their comments too late to be useful. Late contributors to the passaround often are wasting their time reviewing an obsolete version of the work product. I also received some conflicting suggestions, which I had to reconcile.

The passaround helps mitigate two major risks of a peer deskcheck: the reviewer failing to provide timely feedback and the reviewer doing a poor job. At least some of your multiple reviewers will probably respond on time, and several will probably provide valuable input. You can engage more reviewers through a passaround than you can conveniently assemble in a meeting. However, a passaround still lacks the mental stimulation that a group discussion can provide. Once I used a passaround to have other team members review my development plan for a new project. Unfortunately, none of us noticed that some important tasks were missing from my work breakdown structure. We thought of these missing tasks later during a team meeting, which suggests that we would have found them if we had used a team review or inspection instead of the passaround.

As an alternative to distributing physical copies of the document to be reviewed, one of my groups placed an electronic copy of the document in a shared folder on our server. Reviewers were invited to contribute their comments in the form of document annotations, such as Microsoft Word comments or PDF notes, for a set period of time. Then the author reconciled any conflicting inputs from the reviewers, making obvious corrections and ignoring unhelpful suggestions. Only a few issues remained that required the author to sit down with a particular reviewer or two for clarification or brainstorming.

This passaround method allows each reviewer to see the comments that others have already written, which minimizes redundancy and reveals differences of interpretation. Watch out for debates that might take place between reviewers in the form of document comments; those are better handled through direct communication. These document reviews are a good choice when you have reviewers who cannot hold a face-to-face meeting because of geographical separation or scheduling restrictions (see Chapter 12 for other ways to deal with these challenges). Several researchers have developed collaborative tools that extend this simple approach to asynchronous, "virtual" reviewing (Iisakka, Tervonen, and Harjumaa 1999; P. Johnson et al. 1993; P. Johnson 1994, 1996a; Mashayekhi, Feulner, and Riedl 1994). Appendix B contains pointers to some of these tools.

Ad Hoc Review

Chapter 1 opened with a story about one programmer asking another to spend a few minutes helping to track down an elusive bug. Such spur-of-the-moment reviews are a natural part of software team collaboration. They provide a quick way to get another perspective that often finds errors we just cannot see ourselves. Ad hoc reviews are the most informal type of review, having little impact beyond solving the immediate problem.

Choosing a Review Approach

One way to select the most appropriate review method for a given situation is to consider risk: the likelihood that a work product contains defects and the potential for damage if it does. Whether a defect is of major or minor severity depends on its context and the impact it could have if left uncorrected. A small logic error might be a cosmetic irritant if some text is the wrong color but literally fatal in a module that controls a life-support system. Reviews should focus on finding the most severe defects.

Studies have shown that large systems usually contain a small number of error-prone modules. In one system that contained 425 modules, 58 percent of all customer-reported defects resided in only 31 modules (C. Jones 1997). Nearly all of the defects will cluster in just half of the modules, and about 20 percent of the modules will contain about 80 percent of all defects (Boehm and Basili 2001). Factors that contribute to creating error-prone modules include excessive developer schedule pressure, inadequate developer training or experience, and creeping requirements that lead to many changes (C. Jones 1997). Other factors that increase risk include

- Use of new technologies, techniques, or tools
- Complex logic or algorithms that must be correct and optimized
- Mission- or safety-critical portions of the product with severe failure modes or many exception conditions, particularly if they are difficult to trigger during testing
- Key architectural components that provide a base for subsequent product evolution
- Components that are intended to be reused
- Components that will serve as models or templates for other components
- Components with multiple interfaces that affect various parts of the product

Combining informal reviews with inspections provides a powerful quality strategy. During requirements development on one project, we used a series of passarounds to have customer participants informally review the growing requirements specification. The passarounds revealed many errors quickly and cheaply. After we assembled the complete specification from portions written by several analysts, we held a formal inspection, again including key customers. We found an average of 4.5 additional defects per page. Had we not held the informal reviews, we would have had to deal with many more defects during the final inspection, and we certainly would have overlooked other problems in the defect-riddled specification. My quality philosophy is to review such key project documents early and often, both formally and informally, because the cost of finding requirements errors is so much lower in the early stages of the project.

One quality objective is to reduce the risk associated with a given deliverable to an acceptable level. The team should select the cheapest review method that will accomplish this goal. Use inspections for high-risk work products, and rely on cheaper techniques for components having lower risk. You can also choose a review technique based on the stated objectives for the review. Table 3–3 indicates which review approaches are appropriate for achieving specific objectives. The best way to judge which peer review method to use in a given situation is to keep records of review effectiveness and efficiency in your own organization. You might find that inspections work well for code, whereas team reviews or walkthroughs are better for design documents. Hard data provides the most convincing argument, but even subjective records of the types of reviews held, the products examined, and the effectiveness of the reviews will be useful.

Table 3–3. Suggested review methods for meeting various objectives

Review Objectives	Inspection	Team Review	Walkthrough	Pair Programming	Peer Deskcheck	Passaround
Find product defects	X	X	X	X	X	X
Check conformance to specifications	X	X			X	X
Check conformance to standards	X				X	X
Verify product completeness and correctness	X		X			
Assess understandability and maintainability	X	X		X		X
Demonstrate quality of critical or high-risk components	X					
Collect data for process improvement	X	X				
Measure document quality	X					
Educate other team members about the product		X	X	X		X
Reach consensus on an approach		X	X	X		
Ensure that changes or bug fixes were made correctly		X	X		X	
Explore alternative approaches			X	X		
Simulate execution of a program			X			
Minimize review cost					X	

The Inspection Process

Of the several types of software peer reviews, inspections yield the best results. The steps in an inspection provide a thorough quality filter to identify as many defects as possible before baselining a deliverable as a foundation for subsequent work. Inspections also let teams do the following (Gilb 2000):

- Verify that a program possesses desired attributes, such as portability, maintainability, or reusability
- Ensure that stakeholders agree on the technical aspects of a work product
- Gather data on the product and the inspection process
- Enhance the team members' technical skills
- Estimate the number of defects remaining in a work product

This chapter presents an overview of a widely used form of inspection that Michael Fagan (1976, 1986) introduced at IBM in the 1970s to increase programming quality and productivity. Chapters 5 through 8 provide details on the seven inspection process stages. The original inspection method has been enhanced over time (Ebenau and Strauss 1994), and various other types of inspection have been devised to address perceived shortcomings in Fagan's process. Debates continue in the software industry about the best way to perform inspections, whether certain steps can be omitted, and whether all the participant roles are necessary. I address some of those issues in this chapter, but it's more important for your team to begin performing some type of inspection than to endlessly debate the "one true" inspection approach.

Inspector Roles

Members of each inspection team perform several key roles. The most obvious role is that of the *author,* also called the producer or owner. The author usually created the work product being inspected, although he might be maintaining a product that someone else created. Unlike a walkthrough, in which the author typically leads the discussion, the inspection is lead by a *moderator*. The moderator works with the author to plan the inspection, keeps the meetings on track, and leads the inspection team to a successful outcome. Chapter 5 discusses the moderator role in more detail.

The *reader* (also known as the presenter) describes to the other participants the material being inspected during the inspection meeting. Logging the defects, issues, and comments raised during the meeting is the job of the *recorder,* or scribe. The moderator, reader, and recorder are selected from the invited inspectors; they are not additional participants. Any other participants serve as additional inspectors, with no special process responsibilities. The author or moderator might invite certain participants who can examine the work product from specific technical perspectives. At the end of most inspection meetings, a *verifier* might be selected to check the author's rework.

The Author's Role

A fundamental characteristic of inspection is that the author is not permitted to serve as the moderator, reader, or recorder (Ebenau and Strauss 1994). There are several rationales behind this restriction, which is the subject of an ongoing debate. Although the author knows more about the product than anyone else does, he is too close to it to be objective. It's hard for the author to remain egoless if he is controlling the inspection meeting or presenting the material to the other participants. An author who doesn't agree that an issue raised is a defect might elect not to record it. Reporting a possible defect can be more confrontational, and hence uncomfortable for some inspectors, if the author is leading the meeting or performing the reader role.

Another consideration is that giving the author a less active role allows him to listen to the discussion of issues the other participants raise and gain new perspectives about the product. I agree with this point because I've experienced the benefits. During one inspection of some code I had written, an inspector pointed out a particular defect. I was able to quickly find two other instances of the same kind of defect that none of the other inspectors had caught. I found it valuable to listen and think as my coworkers tried to make sense of my program and saw places where I had missed the mark.

This experience also underscored the value of including the author as an inspector. The author has a unique understanding of the product and can sometimes see problems that the other inspectors do not or think of improvements that others hesitate to point out. The author can answer questions about the work product and make sure the recorder logs issues clearly and accurately.

Rather than engage in a debate as to whether the author should take an active role in an inspection, I define "inspection" to include the stipulation that the author may *not* serve as moderator, reader, or recorder. Other types of peer reviews, such as walkthroughs, do place the author in a dominant role, but they are not inspections by this definition.

To Read or Not to Read

Fagan's inspection method uses the role of the reader to present the material being inspected to the other participants in small chunks during the inspection meeting (Ebenau and Strauss 1994). The reader typically paraphrases the work product, stating his interpretation in his own words. The rationale behind using a reader is that someone besides the author tests the understandability of the work product. The reader's interpretation often reveals ambiguities, hidden assumptions, inadequate documentation, style problems that hamper communication, or outright errors. The reader must prepare carefully for the meeting to be able to provide this interpretation.

Many people who perform inspections do not employ a dedicated reader role (Gilb and Graham 1993). Inspectors at Hewlett-Packard concluded that simply having the moderator solicit input on one section of the document after another covered the material faster and improved a well-prepared team's defect-detection rate (Grady and Van Slack 1994). I find that using a reader encourages the inspectors to look more closely at a block of code or set of requirements than they might otherwise. Tori, a colleague of mine, once had a moderator ask her halfway through the meeting to stop trying to put a set of business and interface rules in her own words. The number of comments the other inspectors presented and the number of misinterpretations discovered dropped immediately. The inspection did go faster, but it was not as effective.

While moderating a design inspection, a fellow consultant experienced a vivid illustration of the benefits of using a reader who is not the author:

> *We had three inspectors besides myself and Natalia, who created the design. Jason was a programmer who served as the reader, Sandy was a technical expert who was not assigned to the project, and Mark wrote the requirements specification. While Jason was paraphrasing during the inspection meeting, Natalia interrupted at one point to say, "That was not what I meant." She then explained briefly what she had intended for that section of the design. At this point, Sandy stated that the design Natalia had just described would not work, which took the other inspectors by surprise. Jason and Sandy had both thought that they understood the design and they would have accepted it as is. However, the reading process revealed that Natalia, Jason, and Sandy all had interpreted the design differently. Had the inspection not revealed these differences, Natalia's initial approach would have led to an unworkable design. Natalia spent two weeks rewriting the design document with input from the technical expert, Sandy.*

Reading also gives at least one other inspector—the reader—a good understanding of the author's work. The price you pay for this thoroughness is a slower rate of coverage, which translates into a higher inspection cost. The reading job is difficult, and the reader's own skill and knowledge will limit his ability to present the material clearly. Some people will be more adroit at paraphrasing than others. Rotate the reader role among your team members from one inspection to the next to share the burden of preparing for this challenging function. Rather than dogmatically including or banning readers from your inspections, try performing them both ways and evaluate how well the two methods detect bugs in your team's deliverables.

Inspection Team Size

Keep your inspection teams small, between three and seven participants in most situations. Code inspections usually need only two inspectors besides the author, while inspections of foundational documents such as requirements specifications often demand more inspectors. I like to keep the group small enough that we can all make comfortable eye contact around a table. The four distinct roles suggest that an inspection requires at least four individuals. However, if you have only two participants in addition to the author, the moderator could also serve as either the reader or the recorder. Do not double-up the reader and recorder roles, because they are both quite busy during the inspection meeting.

If the team is too large, distracting side discussions are likely to erupt, which makes it hard for the moderator to control the meeting. If several conversations take place at once, the recorder has difficulty knowing exactly what issues to capture. Large teams also work more slowly than small groups do, so you won't cover the material as fast as you might expect. The more people involved, the harder it is to schedule a meeting, which can delay completing the inspection and therefore impede moving along on the project. Large groups require an assertive moderator to keep the meeting under control.

Some studies have shown that holding multiple parallel inspections with small teams (N-fold inspections) is more cost-effective than using a single large team (Martin and Tsai 1990). An experiment that used nine 3-person teams to inspect the same requirements specification found that the separate teams discovered mostly different errors (Schneider, Martin, and Tsai 1992). When The Boeing Company used several teams to inspect a software standard for safety-critical systems, they discovered that only 14 percent of the defects were found by more than one team (Tripp, Struck, and Pflug 1991). Some studies have concluded that inspections involving only two inspectors besides the author are as effective as using a team with four inspectors (Porter and Votta 1997). This suggests that although the cost of an inspection increases with more participants, the benefits do not increase proportionately. In contrast, though, Bull HN Information Systems found that four-person inspection teams were twice as effective at finding defects and more than twice as efficient as three-person teams (Weller 1993). Such inconsistencies in the published inspection results indicate the need for you to keep records of which approaches work best in your organization.

In general, keep the team as small as you can to meet your inspection objectives while including participants who can find different kinds of defects. Having the right participants, those who will do a great job of finding defects, is more important than including people who will add little value, take the discussion off course, or resent being forced to participate. Using a small inspection team will reduce costs and improve efficiency, but at the price of excluding some interested and possibly valuable participants from the meeting. You might have a small group participate in the inspection meeting and invite additional participants to contribute input through a passaround. Chapter 12 suggests other strategies for handling situations in which many people wish to participate in an inspection.

Inspection Process Stages

Figure 4–1 illustrates the process flow of an inspection, identifying the inspection stages and their participants in the boxes. The heavy arrows show the flow sequence from one process stage to the next. The thin arrows show where each

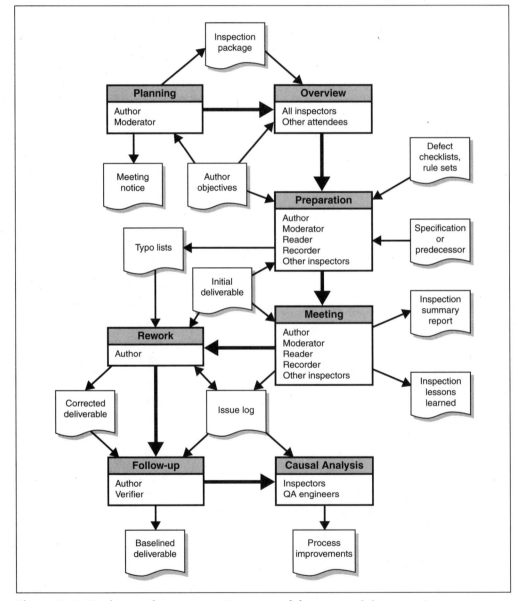

Figure 4–1. The inspection process stages, participants, and documents

document involved in the inspection process is created, used, or updated. Table 4–1 identifies the source of each document and to whom it is delivered.

Fagan (1976) originally described five inspection steps: overview, individual preparation, inspection (the meeting), rework, and follow-up. A discrete planning

Table 4–1. Source and Destination of Inspection Documents

Document	*Comes From*	*Goes To*
Author objectives	Author	Moderator, other inspectors
Meeting notice	Moderator	Inspectors, overview meeting attendees
Inspection package	Moderator, author	Inspectors
Initial deliverable	Author	Inspectors
Defect checklists, rule sets	Process assets library	Inspectors
Specification or predecessor	Author of specification for the initial deliverable or its predecessor document	Inspectors
Typo lists	Inspectors	Author
Issue log	Recorder	Author, moderator, verifier
Corrected deliverable	Author	Verifier
Baselined deliverable	Author	Project's configuration management system
Inspection summary report	Moderator	Peer review coordinator, management
Inspection lessons learned	Moderator	Peer review process owner, peer review coordinator
Process improvements	Inspectors	Organization's software engineering process group

activity prior to the overview is also essential for a successful inspection (Fagan 1986). Experienced inspectors often conclude with a defect causal analysis stage, in which the participants seek to understand the root cause of each defect found and identify ways to prevent future occurrences of similar defects.

In the following sections we look briefly at the essential aspects of each inspection process stage from Figure 4–1. Upcoming chapters describe the stages and their activities in detail. Chapter 5 explores inspection planning. Chapter 6 discusses the overview and preparation stages. The inspection meeting is the topic of Chapter 7, and Chapter 8 addresses rework, follow-up, and causal analysis. Chapter 9 recommends key data items to collect from inspections, metrics to calculate and track, and some approaches for data analysis.

Planning

The author initiates planning by announcing that a deliverable will soon be ready for inspection. First, a moderator is assigned to the inspection. The author's objectives for the inspection help the author and moderator identify people who could provide valuable input and choose specific parts of the deliverable to examine. In addition to the author's objectives, the team or the organization might have specific purposes for inspecting a particular document.

Using the organization's historical data for inspection rates, the moderator estimates the number of inspection meetings that will be needed to cover the material. The moderator is responsible for inviting the other participants. He also schedules the inspection meeting and perhaps an overview meeting. The author and moderator assemble an inspection package that includes the initial deliverable being examined as well as supporting documentation, defect checklists, or other materials. The moderator distributes this package to all inspectors several days prior to the inspection meeting to give them time to prepare.

Overview

The goal of the overview is to enable the inspectors to study the product from perspectives that will reveal defects and satisfy the inspection objectives. The overview is typically conducted through an informal meeting in which the author describes the important features, assumptions, background, and context of the work product. During the overview meeting, the moderator can distribute the inspection package and summarize the inspection process if necessary. Sometimes the author can provide an adequate overview without holding a meeting, by including a short description of the product in the inspection package. If the other participants are already familiar with the work product, you can omit the overview stage.

Preparation

Defect detection begins during the individual preparation stage. During preparation, all inspectors examine the initial deliverable to understand it and to find possible defects and improvement opportunities. Inspectors can use a variety of preparation tools and analysis techniques. A common tool is a checklist that identifies errors that are often made in the kind of work product being inspected. Rule sets define indicators to let you judge whether a work product is complete, correct, and properly constructed. It's also essential to ensure that the initial deliverable actually satisfies its specification and conforms to any applicable standards. Therefore, the inspection package should include—or point to—pertinent specifications, standards, and rule sets for the inspectors to use during preparation.

Preparation is a vital inspection component. If you skip preparation and only hold a meeting, you are essentially conducting a walkthrough, not an inspection. Conversely, performing individual preparation but omitting the meeting is equivalent to a passaround. Walkthroughs and passarounds are valuable peer review techniques, but they are not inspections and they do not discover as many defects.

Meeting

The inspection process centers around collecting defects during the inspection meeting, based on the understanding of the initial deliverable that the inspectors gained during the overview and preparation. During the meeting, the reader describes the work product to the rest of the inspection team, one small portion at a time. After the reader presents each portion, all inspectors can point out possible defects, ask questions, and comment on the work product. The recorder notes each potential defect, suggestion, and issue (point of style, question, or item requiring clarification) on a form in sufficient detail for the author to address it during rework. This *issue log* is the primary deliverable from the inspection meeting. Some people call this deliverable a defect log or defect list, but not every item recorded is an actual defect. The moderator makes sure the meeting remains constructive, watching out for side trips into problem-solving, inappropriate behaviors by attendees, lack of participation, and other problems.

At the meeting's conclusion, the team agrees on an appraisal of the work product. The appraisal could be based on previously established quantitative criteria, such as the extent of rework required or the estimated number of defects that remain in the product. Or it could be a more subjective evaluation of the product's quality, based on the team's experience. The moderator closes the inspection meeting by soliciting input from the other participants about ways the inspection could be improved.

The moderator produces an *inspection summary report* that communicates the work product appraisal and several inspection data items (described in Chapter 9) to the organization's peer review coordinator and to management. Management may not view the issue logs or defect counts from individual inspections, although they may see summary defect information aggregated from multiple inspections. As inspections become institutionalized in your organization, the team members will become more comfortable with having managers view the defect details from individual inspections.

Whether or not a meeting is necessary for an effective inspection is another topic of debate in the software literature (Votta 1993). The rationale for holding an inspection meeting is the potential synergy that results when people put their heads together, discovering new defects that no inspectors found on their own during preparation. However, some research indicates that meeting-based reviews are similar in effectiveness to *asynchronous reviews* that do not include a meeting, in which reviewers contribute comments independently at various times (Porter and Johnson 1997).

Concerns raised about requiring an inspection meeting include delays encountered while attempting to schedule and hold the meeting, participants who arrive late and delay starting the meeting, and the relatively slow coverage of the material being inspected. It can be hard to assemble people for a meeting in a timely way on a fast-moving project. A delay of several days between the time a deliverable is completed and the time the inspection meeting is held can prevent the author from moving ahead with the next step based on that deliverable. Alternatively, if the author does proceed before the inspection results are in, he might have to rework both the initial deliverable and artifacts created from that deliverable. Sometimes this is a sensible risk to take.

A study at AT&T Bell Laboratories concluded that the synergy effect touted as a rationale for holding inspection meetings was actually quite small. An average of only about four percent of the total defects found were discovered during the meeting (Votta 1993). However, this finding does not address some of the less tangible meeting benefits, such as providing learning opportunities for the participants and facilitating technical communication. Learning that other inspectors saw many problems you did not reinforces the fact that one person cannot find all the defects. Experience with Fagan-style inspections suggests that the synergy enhancement is more substantial, with the meeting accounting for perhaps 25 percent of the defects found (Humphrey 1989).

As an alternative to an inspection group meeting, Votta suggests using a series of sequential "depositions": meetings between the author, the moderator, and a single reviewer to log that reviewer's defects. This effectively converts the inspection to a passaround, placing the burden on the author to sit down with the reviewers individually and collate their inputs. As with other challenges to the traditional inspection format, no law says you must hold a meeting during every review. I do not call a peer review that does not involve a meeting an inspection, though.

If you aren't sure whether inspection meetings are suitable for your organization, don't just argue about them—try them! Experiment on real work products to see if your team members conclude that the time they spend in inspection meetings provides a justifiable return. You can measure this return with some simple review metrics on the time invested and the defects found. Also consider the types of defects found with and without meetings. If the meetings don't trigger the "A-ha!" that surfaces a serious error from time to time, and if the team concludes that the intangible meeting benefits aren't that valuable, perhaps inspection meetings aren't important for you. Sometimes, though, scheduling a meeting stimulates more desire to participate in a review than simply asking people to examine a document on their own.

I presented the spectrum of peer review formality in Chapter 3 so you can equip your organization's quality tool kit with multiple review approaches that suit diverse quality goals, work product risks, and resource realities. Thoughtfully considering which situations would benefit from a review meeting makes more sense than demanding either that all peer reviews be inspections or that meetings never be held.

Rework

The inspection isn't over at the end of the meeting. The next step is for the author to address each item on the issue log. The moderator might assign certain issues that arise during the meeting to people other than the author for resolution. While a change might not be necessary in every case, the author should make sure he understands the issue and judge whether or not it is a defect that requires correction. You don't want to lose sight of defects that weren't fixed, only to rediscover them later. Therefore, the author should enter any uncorrected defects in the project's defect tracking system for possible future action. The deliverables from the rework stage are a corrected work product and a marked-up issue log that shows the action taken for each issue and the rationale behind it.

Follow-up

The inspection isn't done until the moderator says it is done. The product appraisal that the team selected at the end of the inspection meeting identified the verification or follow-up step needed to bring closure to the inspection. Typically, the moderator or another designated individual (the verifier) meets with the author to ensure that all issues and defects were resolved appropriately. The verifier also examines the corrected deliverable to confirm that changes were made correctly. Follow-up could involve a reinspection if the team concluded that the magnitude of the rework warranted another close look. After the selected follow-up action is completed, the author baselines the corrected deliverable, checks it into the project's configuration management system, and moves on with his life.

Causal Analysis

As organizations acquire experience performing inspections, they accumulate a body of defect data. Analyzing these defects and assessing how well the team's quality control activities catch them allows the team to improve both its development processes (to prevent defects) and its quality processes (to find defects more efficiently). Causal analysis is performed by organizations that want to maximize the benefits from their inspection data. This is sometimes called the "process brainstorming" stage (Gilb 2000).

One aspect of causal analysis is to understand the root cause behind each discovered defect so you can change the way you create requirements specifications, design descriptions, code, and other project deliverables. Recognizing patterns among the types of defects you find in various work products lets you modify your inspection checklists, analysis methods, and testing approaches to better filter out those defects. As with the other inspection activities, causal analysis is intended to explore shortcomings in the software development processes the team is using, not in the performance of individual team members.

Variations on the Inspection Theme

Not everyone agrees that the classical inspection approach is the best (P. Johnson 1998). Several other types of inspection have been proposed in addition to the method just described (Wheeler, Brykczynski, and Meeson 1996a). Three alternative inspection methods are summarized here.

Gilb/Graham Method

Tom Gilb and Dorothy Graham (1993) developed a rigorous method that emphasizes using inspection to quantify product quality. Measurement is a critical element of their inspection technique because it aids in determining and maximizing the return on investment from inspection. They identify no fewer than 33 inspection data items as being "most important." Gilb and Graham make the accurate point that "If you do not collect and analyze any metrics, you are not doing Inspection! (*their capitalization*) . . ." They also emphasize performing causal analysis of inspection data for process improvement, such that future products are created with lower initial defect levels. Defect prevention is the ultimate reward from an inspection program.

The Gilb/Graham inspection-process stages are similar to those developed by Fagan, but they have different names: kickoff meeting (overview), individual checking (preparation), logging meeting (inspection meeting), and editing (rework). In a notable departure from Fagan's method, Gilb and Graham do not use a reader during the logging meeting. They focus on checking the initial deliverable against its source documents, pertinent rule sets, and checklists, rather than relying on the participants' interpretations of the product to reveal problems.

Organizations are expected to tune their inspections for effectiveness by using optimum checking rates based on data collected from earlier inspections, as well as sets of rules that identify specific defect conditions. The recommended checking rate averages about one full work-product page (300 to 400 words) per hour. This will seem impossibly sluggish to a team confronting a 50-page requirements specification or 10,000 lines of source code. The rationale behind the slow checking rate is that the rewards of finding as many defects per hour as possible outweigh the inspection costs. While this is especially true for work products from the early project stages, the prospect of many hours of inspection might dissuade some teams from trying them at all.

Removing all defects by inspecting the entire product at this slow rate is not economically feasible, yet more rapid coverage will miss many defects. Gilb and Graham recommend evaluating product quality by examining small samples of the product at the optimum rate. Assuming that defects are distributed uniformly throughout the product (although defects are known to cluster in error-prone modules) and that the inspectors were highly effective, a sample provides an estimate of the overall product's quality. The team can then decide whether inspection of the rest of the product is warranted based on numeric criteria for defect densities and return on investment. In addition, the author can often locate additional errors on his own, now that he knows what parts of the product have the most problems and what kinds of problems to look for. Another important idea is to inspect large work products when they are perhaps 10 percent complete rather than waiting until a large body of work has been completed, possibly incorrectly.

The level of rigor that Gilb and Graham describe is laudable and has been demonstrated to be effective (Holland 1999). It might exceed the tolerance for some time-pressured organizations just starting out with peer reviews. Nonetheless, the use of inspection for quantitative document-quality evaluation and defect prevention is the long-term strategic direction that will provide the greatest payback.

High-Impact Inspection

David Gelperin and his colleagues at Software Quality Engineering (1995a) devised an inspection variation termed High-Impact™ Inspection. A briefing stage that either the author or another inspector conducts takes the place of the overview meeting. The briefing addresses the scope and objectives for the deliverable being inspected, its history and rationale, possible usage scenarios, and other topics that will give the inspectors a clear context and background for their examination. The examination step (analogous to individual preparation) is followed by a discussion stage (like an inspection meeting) in which a "guide," who is not the author, focuses the inspectors' attention on four to six critical areas in the product to look for problems.

High-Impact Inspection emphasizes using various analysis techniques to find defects during examination. These methods involve scrutinizing specific aspects of a work product rather than simply asking inspectors to look the product over for problems. The techniques suggested in Software Quality Engineering's HardLook™ Analysis Matrix (part of High-Impact Inspection) include

- *Direct analysis* techniques that look directly at the work product, such as examination for completeness, conformance to standards or syntax, necessity, security, usability, failure modes, and hazards
- *Indirect analysis* of models or other alternative representations of the work product, such as analysis of control flow, data flow, decision logic, state machines, and design coupling and cohesion

Phased Inspections

John C. Knight and E. Ann Myers (1993) developed the phased inspection method to rectify some shortcomings of the classic inspection approach. Phased inspections exemplify a class of peer reviews known as *selected aspect reviews* (Wheeler, Brykczynski, and Meeson 1996a). Phased inspections are a coordinated series of rigorous partial inspections, each of which determines whether a work product possesses a single desired property. These properties could be qualitative (such as portability, reusability, and maintainability) or technical (such as correct use of logical operators in all occurrences). Inspectors use checklists that address only the characteristic being studied. Multiple inspections, perhaps using just one inspector in each, are therefore needed to assess whether a product satisfies all of its desired characteristics. Phased inspections provide a level of rigor that reveals more defects than the usual individual preparation will find, provided that you can define the desired product characteristics through the checklists.

The similarities among these various inspection methods outweigh their differences, so don't spend a lot of energy scouring the literature for the perfect inspection approach. Instead, select one and make it work for you. Properly practiced, any inspection technique will give your team substantial improvements in quality, productivity, and knowledge exchange.

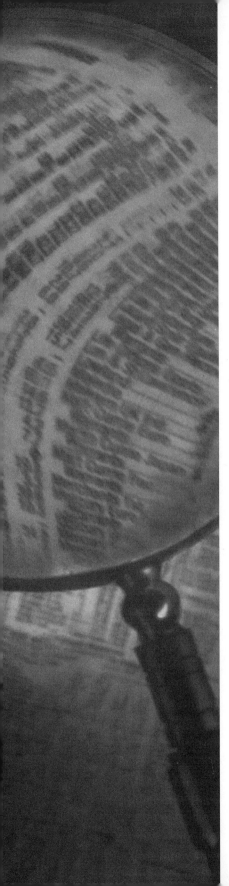

CHAPTER FIVE

Planning the Inspection

One difference between formal peer reviews—such as inspections—and ad hoc reviews is that inspections are planned. At a strategic level, the project manager and quality assurance manager decide which project deliverables need to be reviewed and how to incorporate reviews into the project plan. The project's software quality assurance plan typically defines the peer reviews that will be conducted on the project (IEEE 1999a). Establishing review points provides a sequence of quality gates that keep the project on track. If you don't explicitly schedule formal reviews and allocate time for them, either people won't do them and quality will suffer, or holding the reviews will strain the team's available resources and the schedule could slip.

This chapter describes the activities involved in planning an individual inspection. The first issue is to decide whether you really need an inspection. The author's objectives and the risk associated with the deliverable can help you determine whether a less formal review might be suitable, as discussed in Chapter 3. Your project schedule and quality goals, the work product size, and the availability of suitable reviewers also feed into the decision about which review technique to use. If you decide on an inspection, the author and the moderator need to plan the events and select participants.

Figure 5–1 depicts the inputs, outputs, and participants for the inspection planning stage. The deliverables are a meeting notice that invites participants to the inspection

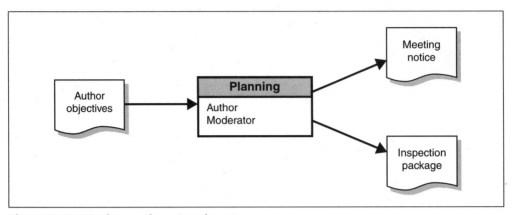

Figure 5–1. The inspection planning stage

events and an inspection package, which is described later in this chapter. Here are the major planning steps:

1. Assign a moderator
2. Select the material to be inspected
3. Judge whether the material is ready to be inspected
4. Choose the inspection participants and assign roles to them
5. Assemble the inspection package
6. Schedule the remaining inspection events

When to Hold Inspections

Plan to inspect a work product when it reaches a completion milestone and is ready to be passed on to the next development step. You can define inspection checkpoints in the project plan even if you don't know yet who the inspectors will be or precisely what artifacts they will examine. If you inspect a deliverable while it is still changing frequently, you'll need to examine it again after it is completed.

Inspections are often viewed as a final quality filter through which a work product must pass before being approved. This is fine, but don't limit inspections to being the ultimate seal of approval. An author should request a peer review whenever he wants feedback on his approach or on specific technical issues. Combine inspections with early or incremental informal reviews for a cost-effective quality approach.

Some development processes involve a series of related documents. For example, requirements development proceeds from a high level of abstraction into progressively more detail. You begin with a vision and scope document that defines the business requirements and then move into user requirements in the form of use cases, business rules, or event tables. These are then elaborated into detailed functional and nonfunctional requirements. Because of the great leverage of correcting early-stage deliverables, plan to inspect all of these requirements documents. Finding an error in a use case is better than learning two months later that numerous functional requirements are wrong because their parent use case was incorrect. One company that began inspecting requirements specifications found that many inspection issues were questions of scope: does a specific requirement even belong in the product? If you resolve scope issues early in the project (perhaps by inspecting your vision and scope document or a project charter), people won't waste time implementing unnecessary requirements.

Plan to inspect the initial increment of a large body of work to look for systemic errors and major misunderstandings. For example, if you're creating a class diagram, inspect an early draft or the first portion of the system that you model to make sure you're on the right track. I once reviewed 5000 lines of C code that one of my team members, Mark, had written. I identified several global changes that would have improved the program's understandability and maintainability, such as replacing literal constants with defined symbolics. However, Mark was too busy to make all of those changes. I wish I had reviewed the first few functions Mark wrote, perhaps 500 lines of code, instead of waiting until he was done to take a close look. That way he could have incorporated my suggestions with just a small amount of effort and followed that improved pattern for the rest of the code.

Figure 5–2 shows that the process of developing, verifying, and reworking a code component could incorporate inspection either before or after unit testing. Prior to unit testing is recommended. First, use the compiler, the linker, and a static code analyzer such as Lint to find errors that tools can catch more efficiently than the human eye can. (The Web site for this book identifies several such static analysis tools; see Appendix B). Then manually inspect the code for logic and problem domain errors before performing systematic unit testing. You could do some limited testing before inspection to smoke out gross errors, but defer comprehensive unit testing until after the inspection is completed.

Novices often begin holding inspections after unit testing. This approach poses several problems (Weller 1993). If you test extensively before you inspect,

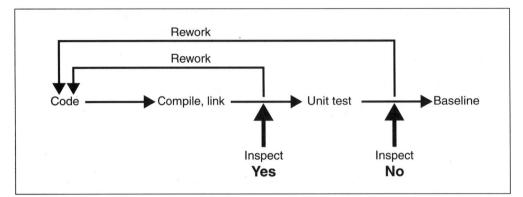

Figure 5–2. Possible points at which to hold a code inspection

you might conclude that inspections don't find many bugs, particularly if you aren't skilled at inspection yet. It's harder to debug test failures than errors found by inspection, because you need to discover the cause of the test failure before you can correct it. Your peers might hesitate to inspect a tested module because it already works. But not all developers are great testers, so a module that appears to work likely still contains bugs.

As an author, you might be reluctant to make some suggested changes because you'll have to do a regression test following rework, retesting the product to make sure the changes did not cause any problems. Inspection might reveal inefficient or excessively complex code, but if you tune up such code, you'll need to retest it. Also, although testing might have to wait until you've implemented a critical mass of related code elements, you can begin inspecting small portions of the code as they are written. Inspections are not a replacement for thorough unit testing, though. The techniques are complementary and reveal different kinds of defects.

The Inspection Moderator

Launching an inspection begins by matching the author with a moderator, or inspection leader. They then select other suitable participants and assign two of them to the roles of recorder and reader. All of your team members should become comfortable with performing the roles of inspector, author, recorder, and reader. The moderator role, however, is more specialized.

The moderator plays a vital role in an effective inspection. One organization found that code inspections led by trained moderators with strong facilitation skills found an average of 39 defects per thousand lines of code, whereas inspections led by untrained moderators detected only nine to twelve defects per thousand lines of code. Effective moderators are well versed in the inspection process, have performed all of the inspection roles themselves, and are committed to the value of inspections. Perhaps most important, they are willing to serve as moderators. Meetings can get away from reluctant moderators who are uncomfortable with steering a group of energetic debaters in a constructive direction. Prospective moderators should receive special training in how to perform this challenging task. Some people are not comfortable leading meetings or correcting their peers' behavior. If such individuals do not want to be inspection moderators, don't force them into this function.

The best moderators share several characteristics:

- They are good at both planning and follow-through.
- They have strong meeting facilitation skills. They start and end on time, set a positive tone, keep the meeting on track, and encourage all participants to contribute.
- They respect the guiding principles for peer reviews from Chapter 2 and do not dominate the meeting with their own comments.
- They are willing to hold people to the guiding principles and to correct inappropriate behavior.
- They are respected by the other participants, who will allow the moderator to manage the meeting.
- They are impartial, fair, and nonjudgmental.
- They have enough technical and domain knowledge to contribute to the inspection.

Every organization needs to develop a pool of qualified moderators. If too few people are willing and able to fill this role, an inspection could be delayed until a moderator is available. Because they have their own project responsibilities, you need enough moderators to avoid overtaxing them. Managers must assure that schedules for people who act as moderators include sufficient time for their inspection commitments. Some organizations rely on their quality assurance department to provide moderators; however, development teams also need to develop this skill internally.

Using a moderator who is not intimately involved with the component being inspected has some advantages. Such moderators are objective and can provide a valuable outside review perspective. However, avoid using nontechnical meeting facilitators to moderate inspections. They might be skilled at keeping meetings on course, but you also want the moderator to contribute to defect detection to get the maximum value for the time invested. Also, do not allow anyone in the author's management chain to moderate an inspection.

There are several ways to select the moderator for a particular inspection (Ebenau and Strauss 1994; Weinberg 2000). In a small group, the moderator role might rotate among the team members so that everyone does the job from time to time. Or, the author might select a moderator from the list of qualified individuals. This lets the author work with someone with whom he is comfortable and someone he knows can contribute to improving the work product. Alternatively, your organization's peer review coordinator's responsibilities might include assigning a moderator to each inspection. If your inspection program is well established, the project manager or QA manager might assign specific moderators to individual inspections during project planning. Regardless of how you select each one, the moderator must be qualified and available.

Selecting the Material

During the planning stage, the author and moderator decide whether to examine the entire deliverable or just selected portions. If the author alone identifies the components to inspect, he could overlook problem areas because he won't be aware of them as potential issues. The author's inspection objectives will help guide the material selection. The quantity of material to be inspected and the organization's recommended inspection rates will help the moderator plan how much time the inspection will take.

Few organizations have the time and commitment to inspect everything they create (unless contractually required to do so), so focus your inspection resources where they will do the most good. If you decide not to examine an entire work product, tell the inspectors which parts you'll cover during the meeting. Look for some friendly folks who are willing to peer-deskcheck the portions you choose not to inspect.

Select the material to inspect based on the risk of its containing errors that could propagate throughout your product and lead to expensive rework or to execution failures. Code that traces back to safety- or security-related requirements should definitely be inspected. Modules in which many changes have been made or which have a history of containing many defects are also good candidates. There is a high probability of making a "bad fix" during rework or adding an enhancement that breaks something else. Horror stories abound about small code changes that sent a spacecraft veering off course or caused similar catastrophes, so no modification is too small to inspect. Nortel Networks found that changes involving up to 30 lines of code had a defect density (the number of defects found per thousand lines of code) about 40 percent greater than that of larger changes (Naccache and Ghaemi 1999). Chapter 3 described several factors that increase the risk of having problems with specific software components. Daniel Freedman (1992) proposed the following additional guidelines for choosing the artifacts to inspect:

- Fundamental and early-stage documents, such as requirements specifications and prototypes
- Documents on which critical decisions are based, such as architectural models that define the interfaces between major system components
- The parts you aren't sure how to do, such as modules that implement unfamiliar or complex algorithms or enforce complicated business rules and other areas in which the developers lack experience or knowledge
- Components that will be used repeatedly

Selective sampling is appropriate for large work products you cannot examine in their entirety or when time is limited. For products that have sections of varying complexity or technical risk, focus your inspection effort on the most complex or risky portions. Inspecting a representative sample of a deliverable provides quality data that will indicate whether you need to inspect the entire deliverable. If your team is skeptical about the value of inspection or overconfident in the quality of their products, examine just a portion and see if their attitudes change. While sampling won't find problems in the sections you don't examine, it can give you clues about the number of residual defects in the product, educate the author, and provide insights into defect patterns (Gilb and Graham 1993). One team that randomly selected three of twenty test cases to inspect found that most of the errors were in the test case preconditions and postconditions. Armed with this knowledge, the author was able to correct many similar defects in the remaining 17 test cases, which was far cheaper than having the entire inspection team discover those defects one at a time.

Inspection Entry Criteria

Entry criteria state the conditions that must be satisfied before you can execute a process with confidence of success. Inspection entry criteria ensure that the work product is in a state that will make the inspection as effective and efficient as possible. The moderator judges whether the initial deliverable satisfies its entry criteria. Proceeding with an inspection when the entry criteria are not fulfilled reduces the likelihood that the team's time will be well spent. These conditions must be met before you begin the inspection process, not just before you hold the inspection meeting. Your team will know you are serious about entry criteria if you postpone inspections whenever they are not satisfied.

One general entry criterion is that all participants have been trained in the inspection process. If the moderator decides to hold an inspection involving untrained novices, he should brief them in advance so they have at least some understanding of inspection. For a reinspection, all issues from the previous inspection must have been resolved. Other entry criteria that apply to most types of work products include the following:

❑ Source documents, specifications, or predecessor deliverables for the item being inspected have themselves passed an inspection and have been baselined. (Inspected products must be verified against these references, and the quality of the output of any step is limited by the quality of its inputs.)

❑ Textual documents have been spell-checked and proofread. (Distracting spelling and grammatical errors can make finding major defects more difficult and take up inspectors' time noting them.)

❑ The initial deliverable has a unique version identifier. (Everyone must inspect the same, known work product.)

❑ The moderator found no flagrant quality problems or layout errors in a brief examination. (Don't waste group time inspecting products you know are badly flawed or lack necessary content.)

❑ The initial deliverable conforms to any applicable standards, templates, or formatting requirements. (Unless the goal of the inspection is to check for such conformance, use this entry criterion to keep inspectors from being distracted by style or formatting issues.)

❑ All open issues are marked by TBD (to be determined). (All TBDs must be resolved before a product is considered complete, but a few TBDs need not hold up an inspection.)

❑ Line numbers are printed on the document or source code listing. (Line numbers help the recorder note the exact location of each problem.)

Your organization should develop objective entry criteria for the various work products you inspect (Gilb and Graham 1993; Gilb 1998). As an example, some additional entry criteria for source code include

❑ The code compiles cleanly with specific compiler switch settings.

❑ Errors found by static code analyzers have been corrected.

❑ The code segments to be inspected have been identified.

Assembling the Cast

Because inspections encompass both technical and social aspects, the success of an inspection depends heavily on who participates. Checklists can help compensate for less experienced inspectors, but people who are skilled at identifying problems will be much in demand. The major guiding principle is to invite people who (a) will provide the most constructive feedback on the work product and (b) are willing to participate. Make it clear that all inspectors are expected to arrive on time and to remain for the full duration of all inspection meetings held.

Be careful when selecting "peers" to participate. Instead of including only people who know the same things the author knows, look for inspectors who have different knowledge and will look at the initial deliverable from other points of view. Programmers often get mired in the minute technical details of the code during an inspection, but people with different perspectives can see the larger picture that reveals erroneous assumptions or functional gaps.

Reluctant inspectors will do only superficial preparation and will add little value. They can also undermine your inspection effort by voicing their disdain for it. However, if you're going to establish a successful inspection program in your organization, every team member must participate. Consider whether interpersonal issues might inhibit the ability of certain individuals to inspect a particular author's work. While we hope that all of our team members can behave in a professional and collaborative manner with their peers, personality conflicts can lead to unpleasant inspection experiences.

Using the same group of inspectors for a set of evolving work products has some advantages. The inspectors will be familiar with the background and context of each new deliverable as it comes up for inspection. However, when you're too close to a work product, you don't look at it as carefully as if it is new to you. It's easy to gloss over defects that have been hanging around undetected for several months, whereas an outsider might question them. Inviting some new inspectors brings a fresh perspective, as well as propagates information about your work products to a larger community. One of my development groups asked people from different projects or even different organizations to participate as an "extra pair of eyes." These inspectors often raised issues the rest of us didn't see and questioned assumptions we had all accepted as truth. Junior team members also bring different points of view. They also learn techniques that will help them do better development work themselves.

Inspector Perspectives

Select inspection participants from the four key perspectives shown in Figure 5–3. Inspectors having these different views, experiences, and interests will spot different kinds of issues. Table 5–1 identifies some project roles that bring these perspectives to the inspection team. You won't be able to represent every role every time because you should normally limit the team to about seven people, including

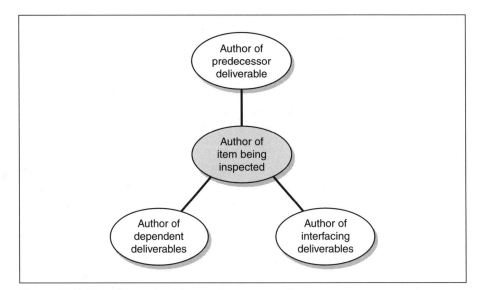

Figure 5–3. Four important inspector perspectives

Table 5–1. Possible Inspectors for Different Types of Work Products

Work Product	_Project Role_
Requirements Specification	Requirements analyst, project manager, architect, designer, system test engineer, quality assurance manager, user or marketing representative, documentation writer, subject matter expert, technical support representative
Architecture Design	Architect, requirements analyst, designer, project manager, integration test engineer
Detail Design	Designer, architect, programmer, integration test engineer
User Interface Design	User interface designer, requirements analyst, user, application domain expert, usability or human factors expert, system test engineer
Source Code	Programmer, designer, unit test engineer, maintainer, requirements analyst, coding standards expert
Test Documentation	Test engineer, programmer (unit testing) or architect (integration testing) or requirements analyst (system testing), quality assurance representative
System Technical Documentation	Author, project manager, maintainer, programmer
User Manual	Documentation writer, requirements analyst, user or marketing representative, system test engineer, maintainer, designer, instructional designer, trainer, technical support representative
Project Plan	Project manager, development manager, business sponsor, marketing or sales representative, technical lead, quality assurance manager
Process Documentation	Software engineering process group leader, process improvement working group members, management-level process owner, practitioners who will use the process

those who are performing the specialized inspection roles. Look for participants who encompass multiple perspectives, such as programmers who are also doing design or quality engineers with extensive testing experience. Sometimes you'll want several representatives of a specific project role, such as two or three users in a requirements inspection.

The most obvious participant is the author. Peers of the author can also be invited. For example, if you're inspecting a requirements specification, include both the analyst who wrote it and a second analyst who can identify poorly written requirements and think of requirements that might be missing. If the original author is not available, the author role is filled by the individual who is currently responsible for the document being inspected.

The second view comes from the author of any predecessor document or specification for the item you're inspecting. For example, if you're inspecting a requirements specification that was based on a marketing document, include the marketing representative who wrote that document. The requirements analyst should participate in a design inspection, and a code inspection team should include the person who designed the modules being inspected. If the same developer both designed and implemented the component, ask the analyst who specified that part of the product, or another designer, to inspect it. When inspecting an enhancement or a modification made in an existing system, invite someone who thoroughly understands the current system to provide this perspective. This understanding will help the person judge whether the necessary changes have been made in every affected part of the product and whether the changes might have adverse impacts elsewhere in the system.

The predecessor perspective is important because one inspection goal is to verify that the work product satisfies its specification. If the most elegant, beautiful, perfect computer program in history doesn't do what it's supposed to do, it is wrong. As you travel back up the development chain, eventually you will reach a requirements document that has no written predecessor. Actual customer representatives or their close surrogates, such as marketing staff, must inspect these documents to validate their contents against actual customer needs. I have seen developers add new requirements during inspections and guess at what a specific requirement means when no customer is in the room to provide definitive answers.

Anyone whose work is based on the item being inspected brings a third important viewpoint. For a requirements inspection, include one of the developers who will design and implement the code and a test engineer who must verify it against the requirements. These potential "victims" of the deliverable will look for problems that prevent them from doing their own jobs, pointing out portions that are hard to understand or are missing information.

The fourth perspective comes from anyone whose deliverables interface with the component being inspected. Routines that handle communications between software components should be inspected by the system architect and by those who developed the components on both sides of the interface. Hardware engineers should inspect software components that interface with sensors, actuators, peripheral devices, or other hardware elements. If you're inspecting a module intended for reuse in multiple products, include representatives from those other project teams to look at the module from their local perspective. One team had a rule that if any of their code changed how a component interacted with the security system, they would not hold an inspection unless someone from the security system team participated.

Consider inviting people who have specialized knowledge that would help them judge whether a deliverable is correct. A requirements inspection could include a representative from manufacturing (in the case of a commercial, mass-market product) or from operations (in the case of a service being offered).

Managers and Observers

The conventional wisdom is that managers may not inspect deliverables created by people who report to them. The rationale behind this restriction is that managers will be tempted to evaluate authors, even subconsciously, based on defects identified during the inspection. A second risk is that other participants might hesitate to point out bugs if they suspect the manager is keeping mental records to use at performance evaluation time. These factors can lead to ineffective inspections and a host of cultural problems.

I believe the issue of whether to include managers in an inspection is less clear-cut than simply saying "No!" Management participation depends on the mutual respect and trust between the manager and the other team members. The author's first-level manager (or other managers who are not in the author's reporting chain) may participate at the author's invitation, provided the manager has the requisite technical knowledge. In small groups, you might need the manager to fill out an inspection team. When I managed a small group, the other team members often invited me to inspect their work. I interpreted this to mean that they respected my experience and ability to improve their products, and they trusted me not to think less of them as professionals if we did find defects. It helps to have a clear statement from the managers that what occurs at inspection meetings will not be used for performance evaluation, although this is a bit like a judge telling the jury to disregard something a witness just said. Without trust and a track record of appropriate behavior, it doesn't matter what the manager says.

Managers need to have their own work products inspected, too. As is the case with many small teams, I still performed technical work when I managed a small development group, and my work was just as subject to inspection as was anyone else's. A technical manager who solicits peer review is leading by example and creating an open culture of constructive criticism and continuous learning. Appropriate stakeholders should inspect deliverables that a manager creates for management purposes, such as project charters, schedules, and development plans. These inspectors could include technical leaders who are organizationally subordinate to the manager, as well as senior managers who might have more project management experience and can help improve the plans.

Limit the presence of observers who do not actively contribute to the inspection. Observers increase the inspection's cost while adding no value to the product. Ask observers to write down their questions instead of asking them during the meeting. Of course, if observers see major defects that no one else mentions, they should speak up. Sometimes people wish to observe the inspection meeting to learn more about the items being examined. Although education is a valuable side benefit of an inspection, consider inviting such interested people to the overview meeting rather than to the inspection meeting. When you are getting started with inspections, be more flexible about allowing observers to attend so they can see how an inspection works. Let people from other groups who are considering starting an inspection process sit in to benefit from your experience. Having new moderators observe an experienced moderator in action is also a valuable learning mechanism.

The Inspection Package

The major deliverable from the planning stage is a package of materials that the author and moderator assemble. The moderator delivers a copy of this package to each inspector prior to the inspection meeting so inspectors have enough time to prepare. The moderator must thread the inspections into the project's work flow. Don't distribute the package for a Monday morning inspection on the previous Friday afternoon, because the participants won't come prepared. You can "include" items in the package by providing pointers to locations where the inspectors can find them, such as on an intranet Web site. After the moderator distributes the inspection package, the author should freeze the work product so it doesn't change prior to the inspection meeting. Typical inspection package contents include the following items:

- The initial deliverable being inspected, with the portions to be examined identified
- Any predecessor documents that define the specifications for this deliverable (for example, design descriptions or models for a code inspection)
- Pertinent standards or other reference documents that will let the inspectors prepare thoroughly
- Any forms the participants will need, such as a typo list or an individual issue log (see Chapter 6)
- Work aids to help the inspectors find defects, such as a checklist of common defects found in this type of work product or rules to which the product is expected to conform
- Test documentation that will be used to verify the initial deliverable

A code inspection package might also include reports from static code analyzers, as well as copies of (or pointers to) other files associated with the source code being inspected, such as header files, makefiles, or code or design descriptions for any collaborating object classes.

Some inspections examine the work product and corresponding test documents together, thereby potentially finding defects in both. Such documents include system test designs or acceptance test cases when you're inspecting requirements specifications, integration tests for architecture and high-level designs, and unit tests for detailed designs and code. Test documentation provides an alternative view of a work product. When you write a test case, you're describing how you expect the system to behave under specific circumstances. Comparing test cases to the product itself often reveals disconnects that indicate an erroneous work product, test case, or both. Including pertinent test documentation in the inspection package encourages early development of the test documentation, shortly after creating the corresponding deliverables. The test documents themselves should undergo peer review, as well.

If you electronically distribute the deliverable being inspected, watch out for formatting differences in the way the inspectors print it. If inspectors print their source listings using different sized fonts or margins or on different paper (such as 8.5 by 11 inches versus A4), their page contents won't match. This is a good reason to print line numbers on both source listings and textual documents. Line numbers make it easy for an inspector to identify the location of a defect, for the recorder to note the location on the issue log, and for the author to find it again during rework. You could also deliver documents in Adobe Portable Document Format (PDF) to ensure that all inspectors are working from the same image.

Inspection Rates

An important part of planning is to judge how much material your team can effectively examine in the time they have available for the inspection. Many organizations have correlated the number of discovered defects with the preparation and inspection rates for different types of work products. These studies find an inverse relationship between the defect density and the preparation and inspection rate, expressed in pages or in lines of code inspected per hour. That is, the more material the team covered in an hour, the fewer defects were discovered per page, as illustrated in Figure 5–4. The pattern could indicate that going more slowly through the material reveals more defects, or it could mean that the

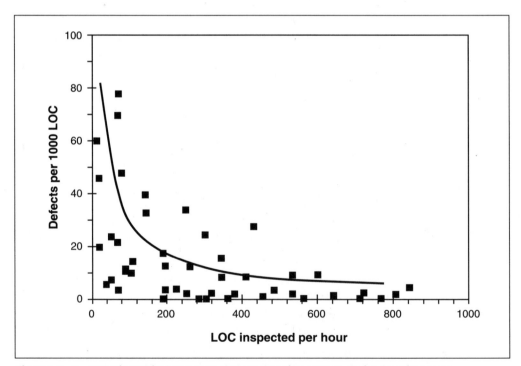

Figure 5–4. Relationship between defect density and code inspection rate

inspection meeting is slowed when the product contains many defects. Both factors probably contribute to the observation.

The published data on optimum inspection rates varies, but the literature data and my own experience suggest that the optimum balance of efficiency and effectiveness occurs in the range of 150 to 200 noncomment, nonblank source code statements per hour. For textual documents such as requirements specifications, design documents, project plans, and process descriptions, aim for a rate of three or four pages per hour. Jalote reported inspection rates for different types of work products measured at Infosys Technologies, Ltd. (Jalote 2000). Adjust these broad guidelines depending on product complexity, criticality, and information density. You can examine the introductory or header portions of documents more rapidly, because they are easier to understand and the errors they contain aren't likely to be serious. Slow down when inspecting convoluted logic, complex algorithms, products in an unfamiliar application domain or coded in a new language, or components in which a failure could have severe consequences.

You can cover more material per hour if it is of low risk, easy to understand, similar to work the team has done before, or contains a low information density per page. A consulting client once balked at my suggestion of inspecting just three or four pages of requirements documentation per hour. I understood their resistance when I saw that their documents had wide margins, large fonts, and generous line spacing. The information content per page was only about half of what I was used to seeing, so they could safely cover more pages per hour than I suggested.

Preparation rates should be similar to the rate at which you cover material in the inspection meeting. The inspectors are unfamiliar with the work product when they examine it on their own, which forces them to read it carefully. However, they aren't slowed down, as they could be during a meeting, by discussions and the need to record details about each issue they see. Gilb and Graham (1993) recommend an optimum individual preparation (checking) rate from 0.5 to 1.5 pages per hour. While this slow checking rate will reveal more errors, it also increases the time the inspection consumes—a price that busy teams might not be willing to pay.

These inspection and preparation rates are averages for planning purposes; individual inspections will of course vary. The team must balance the rate of coverage of the material against the risk of having major defects remain undetected. As your organization gains inspection experience, you can track metrics that include preparation and inspection rates, material size, and defect counts. This data will help you judge appropriate preparation and inspection rates for different kinds of deliverables (see Chapter 9).

The moderator can estimate the meeting time needed from the quantity of material to inspect, your organization's historical inspection rate data, and the author's and moderator's judgment about complexity and risk. A single inspection meeting should not last more than about two hours, so the estimated total meeting time will indicate the number of sessions needed to cover all of the material. Longer meetings will tire the inspectors, making them ineffective and grumpy. If you require more than one meeting, identify the portions you intend to cover in each session so the inspectors can study the right sections at the right time.

Without using inspection rate data during planning, it's easy to try to cover too much material in a single session. You might get through the material, but only by rushing through some of it as you see the clock ticking away during the meeting. Do not proclaim that you completed the inspection if you just skimmed over part of the work product, because you can't judge the quality of the portions you didn't examine closely.

Scheduling Inspection Events

The moderator schedules the events for each inspection. The moderator and author determine whether an overview is needed and, if so, the best way to conduct it.

You can hold the overview meeting as soon as the inspection package is assembled. After the inspection events are selected, the moderator arranges suitable rooms and sends a meeting notice with events, dates, times, and locations to the participants. You might find it convenient to put forms on your company's intranet to help set up inspections, distribute meeting notices and inspection packages by e-mail, and even collect metrics and defect data online. ReviewPro from Software Development Technologies is a commercial tool that provides these, and additional, capabilities.

Some teams allocate a fixed weekly time block—say, Wednesdays from 1 to 3 p.m.—for inspections. This approach does carve out some time in the schedule for inspections, and it reminds the team members that inspections are important and valued by management. However, it is not an ideal solution. If you have work ready to be inspected on Thursday, you have to wait nearly a week before the next inspection opportunity comes up. This could hold up your progress. If your team generates more deliverables in one week than can be inspected in the allocated time, someone's product will be skipped or deferred to the next week. It's impossible to have certain individuals participate in multiple inspections during the week if they all run concurrently. Finally, an author might hastily submit a document for the next inspection window even if it isn't quite ready. Rather than using a fixed inspection schedule, allocate a portion of each week's planned effort for inspections on an average basis, recognizing that some weeks will be busier than others.

Try to schedule the inspection meeting at least one week in advance, and give the inspectors at least two or three business days to prepare for it. Do not have the same team participate in more than one inspection per day; tired inspectors don't find many defects. Don't hold the meeting over lunch in an attempt to save time—you need everyone's undivided attention. If the author and moderator assigned any specific preparation responsibilities to individual inspectors, the moderator should communicate that information when he distributes the inspection package.

Now you're ready to begin the inspection steps that will actually help you improve the quality of your product.

CHAPTER SIX

Examining the Work Product

At the core, an inspection is about examining a deliverable for defects and improvement opportunities. Inspectors conduct their examinations during the preparation and inspection meeting stages. This chapter describes the inspection stages of overview and preparation. The overview stage gives the inspectors enough understanding about the work product so they can commence their bug hunts during preparation.

The Overview Stage

The overview stage (see Figure 6–1) brings all inspection participants up to speed on the scope, purpose, context, history, and rationale of the initial deliverable. You can omit the overview if the inspectors are already acquainted with the initial deliverable. One of my teams did not hold an overview unless the inspectors included non-project participants who were there to bring an outside point of view. An overview meeting is important under the following conditions (NASA 1993; Ebenau and Strauss 1994):

- Earlier versions of the work product have not been inspected.
- A single engineer created the work product.
- Some members of the inspection team aren't familiar with the work product.
- The work product is complex or is tightly interconnected with other system components.

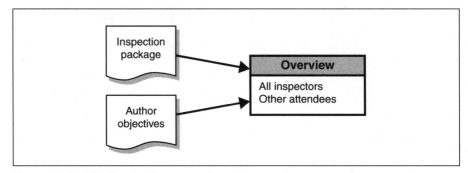

Figure 6–1. The inspection overview stage

- The work product incorporates techniques or technologies that are new to the team.
- The work product provides a critical foundation for subsequent development effort.

The overview often is conducted as a meeting of 30 to 60 minutes in duration, which the author leads. It might be convenient for the moderator to distribute the inspection package to the other inspectors at the overview meeting. A meeting isn't necessary if the author can provide sufficient overview information through a memo in the inspection package, through code comments, or in release notes for a modified component. The overview produces no tangible deliverables, just a shared understanding of the initial deliverable's background and purpose. After the overview, the inspectors can judge whether they understand the work product well enough to scrutinize it on their own. If not, they need some additional information from the author.

The primary goal of the overview is education. If attendees at an overview meeting spot bugs during the author's presentation, they should keep those thoughts to themselves until the inspection meeting. An exception would be if someone saw such a major problem that the inspection should be postponed until the author addresses it. If many interested people wish to learn about the product but you don't want them all to attend the inspection meeting, invite them to the overview meeting instead. This respects their desire to be engaged and shares information with them without compromising the inspection's effectiveness.

The moderator is responsible for scheduling the overview meeting, notifying the attendees, and seeing that the meeting accomplishes its objectives, but the author does most of the talking. The author and moderator determine which presentation approach will be most valuable. For example, the overview for a code inspection should include a general description of what the module does and how it does it. A demonstration is useful in some cases. A code inspection overview might address topics such as:

- The program's operating environment
- Input and output parameters, files, signals, and data streams
- Module preconditions and postconditions
- Exception-handling strategies
- Significant data structures
- Interfaces to users or to other software or hardware components
- Usage scenarios
- Architectural context, perhaps illustrated with design models

The Preparation Stage

The real work of finding problems begins during preparation (Figure 6–2). Recall that the initial deliverable, its specification or predecessor document, and the defect checklists are components of the inspection package. Preparation is so important that if you find a stack of paper on your chair when you arrive at the office at 9:00 A.M. with a note saying "We're inspecting this code at 9:30 today in conference room B," don't even go to the meeting. You aren't prepared and you'll

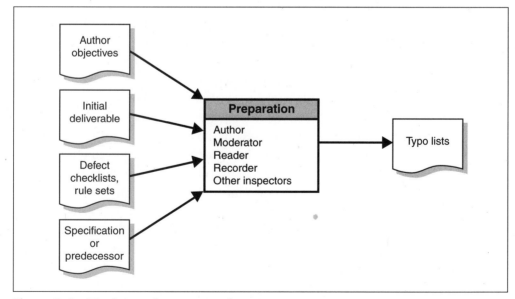

Figure 6–2. The inspection preparation stage

just waste your time. As with overview and inspection meetings, preparation time must be factored into project plans and individual schedules.

During preparation, all inspectors first read through the deliverable to make sure they understand it. Then they examine it for possible errors, using checklists of defects commonly found in that type of work product and other analysis techniques. The inspectors note questions and issues they wish to raise at the inspection meeting. If the moderator assigned special preparation tasks or perspectives to specific inspectors, they examine the product from those points of view.

Some points an inspector wishes to raise about the initial deliverable are defects, while others are simply issues. A defect is a condition that will produce an unsatisfactory result, ranging from a small cosmetic problem to improperly working functionality that could possibly result in loss of data or money, or even life. Chapter 7 presents a simple scheme for classifying defects into various categories. Nondefect issues include questions, points of style, and aspects of the product that need clarification.

Preparation is especially critical for the reader and the recorder. The reader must understand the product well enough to present it to the rest of the team during the inspection meeting. The reader often brings notes to the inspection meeting that summarize the key points he wants to make about each section of the product. The recorder is also busy during the meeting, capturing the salient points of each issue raised. It can be hard for the recorder to think about the work product during the meeting, so he needs to come prepared with the issues he wants to bring up. Sometimes the recorder asks another inspector to present his comments so he can stay focused on the recording task.

While most people simply jot notes on the work product itself during preparation, some organizations have inspectors record the issues and defects they find on a personal issue log (Jalote 2000). This provides a complete record of the inspector's observations, including additional detail that the inspector can impart to the author without consuming meeting time. It helps with the problem of using less skilled recorders or biased recorders who don't accurately capture points raised during the meeting. One of my colleagues found that using personal issue logs made the meetings go faster, the recorder's job easier, and the author's rework tasks clearer. Her team also used the individual logs to collect descriptions of individual fixes and for rework verification. The tradeoff (there is always a tradeoff) is some additional effort by the inspectors to create the logs and effort by the moderator or author to collate the contents of multiple issue logs.

The inspectors can note minor items such as typographical errors, misspellings, and formatting problems on the *typo list* shown in Figure 6–3 and hand these forms to the author at or before the inspection meeting. (The typo list and other inspection forms are available for downloading from the Web site that supports this book; see Appendix B.) Using a typo list is more efficient than spending time on such small issues during the meeting. It's also less confusing for the author than giving him several marked-up copies of the initial deliverable with some items having been logged during the meeting and others not. Ordinary typos are not counted as defects found during the inspection. Sometimes, though, a typographical error can completely change a requirement, such that a code module would be implemented incorrectly. Those are indeed defects.

Some inspection authorities recommend against separating typos from other defects. The concern is that if typographical errors are not regarded as defects, they might become viewed as being acceptable and authors might become sloppy about proofreading their work. If this becomes a problem for you, count typos as defects to encourage people to take them seriously.

Each inspector records how much time he spends on preparation, and the moderator collects those times at the beginning of the inspection meeting. If the moderator judges that some inspectors are not adequately prepared, he reschedules

---

Inspection Typo List

Record any typographical errors you find during your inspection preparation on this list, including spelling, grammatical, formatting, and style errors. These should be corrected but need not be discussed at the inspection meeting. They will not be counted as defects.

Inspector: _____

Scheduled Inspection Meeting Date: _____

Work Product Identification: _____

Page Number	Line Number or Section	Description of Typo
_____	_____	_____
_____	_____	_____
_____	_____	_____
_____	_____	_____
_____	_____	_____

Figure 6–3. Inspection typo list

the meeting to allow more preparation time. One guideline I use is that preparation time should approximately equal the planned meeting duration. Preparation time can be considerably longer than the meeting time if you're examining complex or unfamiliar products or if the inspectors are using multiple analysis techniques. A long-term study of code inspections conducted as part of the National Software Quality Experiment found that the average preparation time was 2.6 times the meeting duration (O'Neill 2001). However, other experiences indicate that preparation rates can be somewhat faster than inspection rates (Jalote 2000).

Some organizations use a "study hall" approach, in which the participants prepare immediately following the overview meeting in the same room in which the overview was held. This is convenient because the inspectors are all in one place and the work product's background is fresh in their minds. More typically, though, the inspectors examine the initial deliverable on their own time between the overview and the inspection meeting a few days later.

The author needs less preparation time than the other inspectors do, although he should still prepare. If you set aside something you created for a day or two and then look carefully at it, you will find errors on your own. When I'm writing, I don't review a completed article or book chapter for at least a day. The mental settling time helps me look at the work more objectively. If the author has conducted a careful personal deskcheck, using a defect checklist, before requesting the inspection, he need not perform additional preparation.

Inspectors sometimes come up with questions for the author during preparation. Avoid discussing these prior to the inspection meeting unless deferring them would interfere with proper preparation. If discussions between an inspector and the author do take place, the author should communicate the answers to questions raised to all of the inspectors.

Preparation Approaches

Many people prepare by starting at the first line of the document being inspected and reading through it sequentially, noting anything that looks suspect. However, effective inspectors will go through the material several times, focusing on a different product aspect during each pass. This increases the number of defects they find at the expense of also increasing the preparation time. If you have enough time, wait a few hours between passes for your mind to clear. Otherwise, it's easy to retrace your thought process from the previous examination, perhaps looking right at errors without seeing them.

Rather than leaving the preparation mode up to each individual, some moderators recommend suitable analysis strategies for each inspector. This reduces redundant effort and targets specific areas of concern. The moderator can assign certain preparation objectives to specific inspectors to exploit their specialized technical knowledge or to ensure that all checklist items are addressed. The author's inspection goals will dictate some such preparation objectives.

Suppose you're inspecting a requirements specification that includes a complex state-transition diagram and its associated functional requirements. The author might want one inspector to ensure that no states or transitions are missing, superfluous, or incorrect. Another inspector could ensure that the diagram accurately maps to those functional requirements that describe the state machine's behavior in detail. Some other focused preparation activities to consider assigning to individual inspectors include:

- Checking all internal and external cross-references
- Checking interfaces for correctness
- Checking for consistency on variable names or domain-specific terminology
- Seeing whether the work product conforms to pertinent standards, templates, or rules
- Verifying that the deliverable satisfies its specification, conforms to all pertinent predecessor documents, and does not contain unnecessary elements
- Evaluating testability or checking the product against its test documentation

You don't want everyone to look closely at the first one-third of a large work product, a few to get to the middle third, and just one stalwart inspector to flip through the final portion. If it's logically appropriate, ask inspectors to begin their examination at different points in the deliverable. At least one person should read the entire product for continuity issues, such as inconsistencies between requirements. One disadvantage of having inspectors prepare in different ways is that you must rely on all of them to prepare effectively, because there is no redundancy on which to fall back.

Defect Checklists

Checklists that identify typical defects found in various software work products are an important part of an organization's inspection infrastructure. Checklists help the inspectors focus their attention during preparation on likely sources of errors that could cause program failures. They also help the team members build better products by knowing in advance what kinds of problems to avoid. You can create checklists to direct an inspector's attention to specific issues in a product, such as judging conformance to a specific industry or government standard.

Checklists are usually written in the form of questions for the inspector to ask about the deliverable he is examining, grouped into logical categories. Figure 6–4 illustrates a checklist for inspecting a project plan. This example indicates that an inspector needs a copy of pertinent project plan standards, procedures, or templates to evaluate certain checklist items.

Either keep the checklists short, or group checklist items into several categories. An inspector can keep only about half a dozen individual checklist items in mind when analyzing a document. If the list contains many more items than that, the inspector must make multiple passes through the document, looking for a different set of problems on each pass. To increase efficiency, the moderator could ask different inspectors to use different groups of checklist items. Don't include items on checklists for problems that compilers and static code analyzers can find. Rather than inventing your own, start with the defect checklists on the Web site for this book. As you learn what kinds of problems recur in your own deliverables, tailor these checklists to meet your specific needs.

Rule Sets

As a supplement or alternative to using checklists, inspectors should look for violations of rules for the kind of work product being inspected. *Rules* are statements that direct authors to perform tasks or construct product documents in a particular way (Gilb and Graham 1993). Rules can address document contents, structure, notations, or organization. They might define conventions for naming objects, formatting source code, organizing a document, or tracing objects to their sources. As with checklists, you can create your own rule sets, or you can start with examples such as those provided in Appendix D of Gilb and Graham's *Software Inspection* book (1993).

Rule sets provide an objective way for an inspector to judge whether a work product is correct and complete. For example, requirements specifications should be complete, consistent, correct, feasible, modifiable, necessary, prioritized, traceable, unambiguous, and verifiable (Wiegers 1999). Rule violations are defects. Demonstrating that a work product violates a specific rule is a more palatable way to point out a defect than arguing over personal preferences or matters of opinion.

Other Analysis Techniques

Selecting appropriate analysis techniques from a palette of options is more powerful than always using checklists or just reading through the work product. Your inspection analysis methods should reveal errors that are hard to discover

---

Checklist for Project Plan Inspections

Clarity

❑ Is the project plan appropriately composed, being neither too detailed nor too general?

❑ Is the meaning of each plan component clear and unambiguous?

❑ Is the relationship between plan components clear?

❑ Is the plan organized in a logical and clear way and consistent with an applicable template?

Completeness

❑ Are all estimates documented, along with the method used for deriving them?

❑ Does the project plan include all the items required by the applicable standard, procedure, or template?

❑ Are relevant details missing from any plan components?

❑ Are irrelevant details present in any plan components?

❑ Are some plan components unnecessary?

❑ Does any information appear redundantly in the plan?

❑ Are all related or reference documents listed?

Consistency

❑ Are related components within the plan consistent with each other?

❑ Is the content of the plan consistent with the contents of all related documents?

❑ Is the content consistent with the project's scope and objectives?

❑ Is the level of detail, vocabulary, and syntax in the document consistent with its audience and usage assumptions?

Correctness

❑ Are any tasks missing from the work breakdown structure?

❑ Are all estimates realistically achievable?

❑ Are all assumptions that went into project planning stated and accurate?

Figure 6–4. Checklist for project plan inspections

through testing. A risk assessment of the product's possible failure modes will suggest suitable inspection analysis strategies. Using traceability to check for completeness is a valuable analysis step for all software deliverables (O'Neill

2001). Verify that all product components can be linked back to specific require-ments (there are no orphans) and that all requirements have been traced into designs, code, and other elements (nothing has been overlooked). Other analysis strategies are described below for several major project deliverables. Many of these methods engage the inspectors actively during preparation, in contrast to unstructured and checklist-based preparation approaches.

Requirements Specifications. Evaluating requirements for testability re-veals incomplete, ambiguous, and inconsistent requirements (Drabick 1999). Some tools are available that scan requirements documents for keywords that indicate vagueness or ambiguity. One such product is the Automated Require-ment Measurement (ARM) Tool, available at no charge from the Software Assurance Technology Center at the NASA Goddard Space Flight Center (see the Web site accompanying this book). Some commercial requirements manage-ment tools, such as Caliber-RM from Starbase Corporation, also feature ambigu-ity checking.

Perspective-based reading (PBR) defines steps that inspectors can follow when reading a specific type of document to improve their understanding of it and look for problems (Basili et al. 1996; Shull, Rus, and Basili 2000). With PBR, individual inspectors read a requirements specification from the perspective of different users of the document. One inspector might read the specification from the customer's point of view, another from the designer's perspective, and a third as a system tester. Ideally, the actual team members who fill those roles will participate in the inspection, the customer representative being particularly important.

The PBR procedure presents questions that help inspectors judge how suit-able each document is for its intended purpose. A PBR procedure could also specify activities that the inspector should perform to evaluate the product's completeness or correctness, such as developing a set of test cases from the speci-fication. These activities take more time than traditional inspection preparation, but they are also more rigorous and comprehensive.

Scenarios are a related analysis technique for requirements specifications (Porter et al. 1995). Scenarios are procedures that help inspectors find specific types of defects, such as missing requirements, inconsistencies, ambiguities, or incorrect functionality. Some scenarios ask thought-provoking questions that the inspector must answer. Others direct the inspector to perform specific tasks with the work product, such as identifying all output data items for a specific require-ment and listing at least one requirement that uses each of these data items as input. Giving different inspectors separate scenarios provides a broad coverage that finds orthogonal sets of defects, so having multiple inspectors adds more value with less redundancy. In one experiment, Porter and Votta (1997) concluded that the scenario approach revealed more defects than did using either checklists or an ad hoc preparation approach, which both gave similar results. However, other experiments have not confirmed the superiority of scenarios (Sandahl et al. 1998).

Missing requirements are among the most difficult requirement problems to detect. They aren't in the specification, so the inspectors don't see them during preparation and the reader doesn't describe them during the inspection meeting. Use the following techniques to look for missing requirements:

- See if you've received requirements from all of your product's identified user classes.
- Examine similar and competing products for additional functionality.
- Check whether nonfunctional requirements, such as quality attributes, performance goals, constraints, and external interface requirements, have been specified.
- Ensure that the specification conforms to all pertinent business rules.
- Represent requirements information in multiple ways, including structured text and graphical analysis models. Analysis and design modeling notations include data flow diagrams, entity-relationship diagrams, state-transition diagrams, class diagrams, and other object-oriented models that are defined in the Unified Modeling Language (Booch, Rumbaugh, and Jacobson 1999).
- Build tables of similar requirements that fit a pattern to avoid duplications or oversights (Wiegers 1999).
- Create a checklist of typical functional categories for your products, such as reporting, edit operations, security, user customization, printing, transaction logging, and so on. During preparation, see if requirements are present in all pertinent categories.
- State the source and usage of all data items.

An inspection that identifies unnecessary requirements pays for itself by reducing the project's development effort. One of my consulting clients held a requirements inspection that saved at least one month of engineering effort. The inspection revealed that simply providing several report templates could replace the custom report generator that was originally specified. The product implementation was outsourced to a company in a country whose culture expected developers to build exactly what was specified without asking any questions. Had the inspection not been held, the unnecessary custom report generator would have been noticed only after it had been completed by the developing company—an expensive error.

User Interface Designs. Inspections can be applied to screen shots, prototypes, paper prototypes, and user interface architecture designs such as dialog maps (Wiegers 1999). Jakob Nielsen (1993) developed the *heuristic evaluation* method, in which inspectors evaluate a user interface design against a set of heuristics, or rules, for effective interface design (Nielsen and Mack 1994). Constantine and Lockwood (1999) described a *collaborative usability inspection* technique that a team can use to search for usability defects in any software deliverable. In the first inspection stage, the team walks through both typical and exceptional usage scenarios to identify problems in the way users would interact with the system. A second pass through the user interface examines every display for problems with controls, icons, screen layout, colors, buttons, prompts, and the myriad other elements of user interface design. A related analysis activity searches for inconsistencies in the appearance, terminology, navigation, or functioning of user interface elements. These techniques can greatly improve the most visible part of a software application, the user interface.

Design Documents. System architectures can be reviewed by using scenario-based, questionnaire-based, or checklist-based techniques (Bass, Clements, and Kazman 1998). Parnas and Weiss (1985) developed the *active design review* as an improvement on the traditional checklist of questions that prompt for yes-or-no answers. Each participant in an active design review receives a different checklist, so the reviewers are looking at different aspects of the product for problems. The checklist items are open-ended and again stimulate the reviewer to be actively engaged during preparation. Examples of active design-review checklist items are "Write down the exceptions that can occur for each module" and "State the range or set of legal values of each parameter." If you can't perform these tasks, the design has some problems.

Source Code. Considerable research has been devoted to ways people can read source code for maximum comprehension. Active design reviews apply to code as well as to designs. Rather than reading sequentially through the code listing, inspectors traverse the hierarchical structure of the code, following function calls down the call tree as they are encountered (Parnas and Weiss 1985). Inspectors proceed systematically through the code so that no section of the program gets overlooked. Inspectors should analyze exception-handling code carefully, as it is often difficult to trigger all exception conditions during testing.

Another code analysis technique involves building visual models that represent the program's functions at a higher level of abstraction. If you can't create accurate and consistent models from the code, the code contains errors, is missing necessary elements, or is too confusing. Decision tables and trees help ensure that the program handles every condition. A control flowgraph shows the branching logic in a code module (Beizer 1990). Even creating a simple flowchart from the code might reveal missing or incorrect logic. Various commercial computer-aided software engineering tools can generate some of these models from source code or can analyze code for conformance to specified programming practices and rules. See Appendix B for pointers to some of these tools.

Inspectors can analyze both designs and code for desired quality attributes that otherwise can be evaluated only in product operation. Specifying these attributes during requirements development allows developers to make design choices to achieve the stated quality goals (Wiegers 1999). Some of these attributes are difficult to measure objectively, so the judgment of the inspectors is necessary when evaluating whether a product satisfies its quality goals. Some quality attributes that are important to many products include:

- *Maintainability.* How easily can another programmer understand and modify the code? Is it well-structured and adequately documented?
- *Robustness.* How will the product respond under unanticipated operating conditions? Are defaults specified for incorrect or missing inputs?
- *Reliability.* Is it fault-tolerant? Does it have effective exception-handling and error-recovery mechanisms?
- *Efficiency.* How much memory or processor capacity does the program consume? Are algorithms optimized and unnecessary operations avoided?
- *Reusability.* Can components be reused in other applications? Does the program have a well-partitioned, modular design with strong cohesion and loose coupling?
- *Integrity.* Does the system protect software and data from unauthorized access, loss, modification, and virus infection?
- *Scalability.* Can the system grow to accommodate more users, servers, data, or other components at acceptable performance and cost?

Walking through test designs or test cases is a powerful analysis technique for requirements, designs, and code. You should inspect the test plans, designs, cases, and procedures in their own right. The test documentation then helps you hunt for defects in the other work products. Look for disconnects between your mental vision of how the system should behave, as captured in the tests, and the functionality you actually intend to build, as defined in the requirements. Make sure all the functional requirements map to individual test cases, and ensure that each test case can be "executed" with the set of functional requirements in the specification.

Any systematic analysis techniques you can apply during individual preparation will help you find the tough defects that casual reading doesn't reveal. Careful individual preparation lays the foundation for a successful inspection meeting.

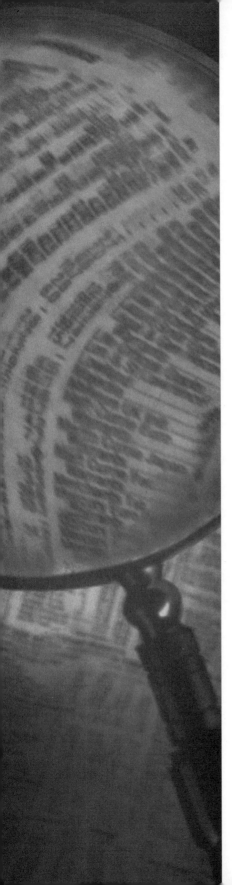

CHAPTER SEVEN

Putting Your Heads Together

The inspection meeting is the heart of the inspection. In the meeting, the inspectors carefully examine the initial deliverable as a group, led by the reader. As they go through the product, they identify defects and other issues, which the recorder notes on an issue log. One inspector's comment often triggers another's insight, which leads to additional defect discovery. With the moderator's guidance, they avoid getting sidetracked on unproductive discussions. And, the inspectors treat the author and the work product with respect.

If all goes well, a two-hour inspection meeting will result in a higher-quality deliverable than the author could create on his own. However, a meeting that turns into a blamefest, spends more time solving problems than finding them, or fails to cover the material thoroughly is wasteful and frustrating. It's up to the team, and especially the moderator, to make each inspection meeting a positive experience. As shown in Figure 7–1, the meeting deliverables include the issue log, an inspection summary report that identifies the participants and other inspection parameters, and lessons learned that suggest ways to improve the inspection process.

The Moderator's Role

The moderator leads the inspection meeting and plays a major part in a successful inspection (Jalote 2000). He keeps the meeting on track, controls the pace, keeps the participants effectively engaged, and leads the team to an appraisal of the work product's quality. Most inspection meeting

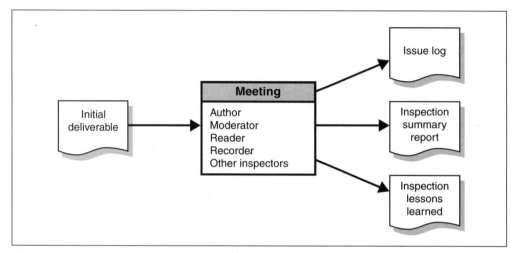

Figure 7–1. The inspection meeting stage

problems reflect shortcomings in moderator performance. Poorly moderated inspections can degenerate into unstructured discussions that fail to meet the inspection's goals. Figure 7–2 shows a checklist to remind the moderator how to prepare for, launch, close, and follow up on the inspection meeting. You can

---

Inspection Moderator's Checklist

Things to Bring to the Inspection Meeting

❑ Inspection summary report with inspection identification, work product description, inspector names and roles, pages or lines of code planned for inspection, total overview effort, and planning effort filled in.

❑ Typo list for participants to share to note additional small items spotted during the meeting.

❑ Issue log for the recorder.

❑ Inspection Lessons Learned questionnaire.

❑ Attention-getting device.

❑ Paper for action items and other issues that come up.

❑ Appropriate work product defect checklist or rule set.

❑ For a reinspection, the issues list from the previous inspection.

(continued)

Figure 7–2. Inspection moderator's checklist

At the Start of the Inspection Meeting

❏ Perform introductions if participants do not all know each other.

❏ Identify the author and the individuals performing the reader and recorder roles.

❏ Announce the work product being inspected and state the author's inspection objectives.

❏ *Say:* The author has created this product and asked us to help make it better. Please focus your comments on improving the product.

❏ *Say:* Look beneath the superficial minor defects or style issues you see to hunt out significant defects. If you aren't sure if something is a defect, point it out and we'll decide as a team.

❏ *Say:* Our goal is to identify defects, not devise solutions. In general, I will permit about one minute of discussion on an issue to see if it can be resolved quickly. If not, I will ask that it be recorded and we'll move on to try to find additional defects.

❏ *Say:* If anyone spots a typo or small cosmetic problem, please record it on the typo list rather than bringing it up in the discussion.

❏ *Say:* Let's have only one person speaking at a time so there aren't multiple meetings going on simultaneously.

❏ Explain any attention-getting device you will use. Ask inspectors to respect your interruptions and yield the floor to you.

❏ *Ask the author:* If the inspectors have the current version of the document or whether he has made any significant changes that might affect the inspection.

❏ *Say:* At the end of the meeting, we'll decide what our appraisal of this product is: accepted as is, accepted conditionally upon verification, reinspection needed, or inspection not completed. Describe how the group will make the appraisal decision.

❏ *Say:* We'll take a few minutes to discuss lessons learned from the inspection at the end of the meeting.

❏ *Ask the inspectors:* If they have any questions.

❏ Record everyone's preparation time on the inspection summary report and add them to get the total preparation effort. Judge whether it is sufficient to proceed with the meeting or whether you should reschedule it.

(continued)

Figure 7–2. Inspection moderator's checklist (*cont.*)

❑ *Ask the inspectors:* For any positive comments they wish to make about the initial deliverable.

❑ *Ask the inspectors:* For any global observations that pertain to the entire document.

❑ *Ask the reader:* To begin.

At the End of the Inspection Meeting

❑ Lead the team to a product appraisal and record it on the inspection summary report.

❑ If the appraisal was "accept conditionally," determine who will do follow-up verification, and write his or her name on the inspection summary report.

❑ Record the actual pages or lines of code inspected.

❑ Collect lessons learned from this inspection.

❑ Remind inspectors to pass their typo lists to the author before they leave.

❑ Provide copies of the issue log to the author and verifier.

❑ Record the meeting time on the inspection summary report.

❑ If a separate list of action items was generated, deliver it to the appropriate individual(s).

After Rework Is Completed

❑ Obtain from the author the actual rework time, the total number of major and minor defects found, and the number of major and minor defects corrected. Record the rework time on the inspection summary report.

❑ Give the inspection summary report and the summary defect metrics to the peer review coordinator. If the coordinator needs defect details to enter into the inspection database, also give him the issue log.

Figure 7–2. Inspection moderator's checklist (*cont.*)

download this checklist and the other work aids described in this chapter from the Web site for this book.

The moderator's worksheet is the inspection summary report, illustrated in Figure 7–3 (Freedman and Weinberg 1990; Wiegers 1996a). Summary reports become part of the documentation for each project that conducts inspections. The report contains information that feeds into the organization's inspection database. You can use this form for any type of peer review for which you wish to keep records, not only for inspections. Tailor it, and all the other materials described here, to meet your organization's needs best.

Inspection Summary Report

Inspection Identification

Project: _____

Inspection ID: _____

Meeting Date: _____

Work Product Description:

_____

_____

	Inspectors	Signature	Preparation Time

1. Author: _____ _____ _____ hours

2. Moderator: _____ _____ _____ hours

3. Recorder: _____ _____ _____ hours

4. Reader: _____ _____ _____ hours

5. Inspector: _____ _____ _____ hours

6. Inspector: _____ _____ _____ hours

7. Inspector: _____ _____ _____ hours

Inspection Data

☐ Pages or ☐ Lines of Code   Meeting Time: _____ hours

Planned for Inspection: _____   Total Planning Effort: _____ labor hours

Actually Inspected: _____   Total Overview Effort: _____ labor hours

Total Preparation Effort: _____ labor hours

Actual Rework Effort: _____ labor hours

Product Appraisal

ACCEPTED   NOT ACCEPTED

_____ As is   _____ Reinspect following rework

_____ Conditionally upon verification   _____ Inspection not completed

Verifier: _____

Projected Rework Completion Date: _____

Figure 7–3. Inspection summary report

The Inspection Identification section of the summary report uniquely identifies each inspection. I use a simple identification scheme for each project's inspections, with the document type (REQS, CODE, TEST, and so on) followed by a sequence number. For example, DESIGN-4 is the fourth design inspection held on a particular project. Briefly describe the deliverable being inspected in the Work Product Description section. The summary report also identifies the inspection participants and their inspection roles.

The moderator records several data items on the inspection summary report, including the following:

- Quantity of material (pages or lines of code) that you planned to inspect and that was actually inspected
- Inspection meeting duration
- Total effort that the moderator and author spent assembling the inspection package and performing other planning activities
- Total overview meeting effort if one was held (meeting duration in hours multiplied by number of participants)
- Hours each inspector spent on preparation and the team's total preparation effort
- Actual rework effort (unknown until the follow-up stage)

Inspection measurements such as these (discussed further in Chapter 9) let the organization determine each inspection's cost, plan time allocation for future inspections, and judge whether the inspection was a cost-effective investment in quality. The summary report also identifies the team's appraisal of the work product, which is described later in this chapter. If verification is required following rework, name the designated verifier on the summary report. Setting a target date for completing rework helps motivate authors to complete this critical step in a timely fashion and brings the inspection to closure.

Launching the Meeting

The moderator begins the meeting by introducing the participants if they don't already know each other and announcing who is performing each inspection role. He identifies the work product being inspected and recaps the author's inspection objectives. It doesn't hurt to remind the participants that the inspection's purpose is to find defects and otherwise improve the product. The moderator asks the other inspectors to note any small errors they see on a typo list to be passed to the author at the end of the meeting. If participants have questions about the item being inspected or about the inspection itself, now is the time to ask them. The moderator also asks if the author has changed the initial deliverable since it was distributed. Significant changes might negate some of the preparation effort.

Periodically during the meeting, the moderator might need to interrupt the discussion to refocus the group or curtail problem-solving. To get the team's attention when he needs the floor, the moderator could wave a piece of colored paper or a small flag, bang a gavel, or—more whimsically—hold up a rubber chicken (why can't inspections be fun?). The moderator should explain his attention-getting device at the beginning of the meeting and ask the participants to respect his need to gain control of the discussion from time to time.

Next, the moderator asks all inspectors how much time they spent on preparation and records these times on the inspection summary report. If participants are uncomfortable sharing their preparation times publicly, they can pass them to the moderator on paper. Recall that the preparation time should approximate the planned inspection meeting time. The moderator can also ask inspectors if they feel adequately prepared to proceed. If not, perhaps the overview was inadequate or they did not receive the inspection package early enough to spend time on preparation. If the moderator judges that some participants are not properly prepared, he has the authority—and the responsibility—to reschedule the meeting. Proceeding with unprepared participants wastes time and undermines the inspection's effectiveness.

Judging preparedness is subjective, and it takes courage for the moderator to terminate the meeting. A fellow consultant once watched a developer named Jack moderate an inspection of a new coding standards document. When Jack asked if everyone had read the draft standard, one developer replied, "No, I didn't have time." Jack immediately cancelled the meeting and said he would reschedule it to be held within the next two days. From then on, everyone came well-prepared for all inspections. Jack didn't insult the unprepared developer, but his clear commitment to adequate preparation, coupled with peer pressure to complete the inspections expeditiously, did the trick. The unprepared developer had a history of sloppiness, which changed dramatically after this small but seminal event.

I sometimes judge preparation adequacy by seeing how many items the inspectors wrote on their personal issue logs and typo lists or how many notes they have made on the work product itself. Products that aren't marked up could simply mean that the work product is in good shape, or it could mean that the inspector didn't look carefully. To encourage careful preparation, consultant Brian Lawrence recommends choosing the reader and recorder at the beginning of the inspection meeting. Every inspector therefore must prepare as if he might have to present the material to the others. Although this approach encourages thorough preparation by all participants, it places a larger preparation time burden on those inspectors who will not have the reader role. Ultimately, you must rely upon the professionalism of your team members to prepare properly. Once the inspection culture is firmly established in a team, inadequate preparation should not be a problem.

In some organizations, inspectors submit personal issue logs or a count of the defects they found to the moderator prior to the meeting. This procedure alone often encourages participants to prepare carefully (Genuchten et al. 2001). From this information, the moderator can judge whether preparation appears adequate. The moderator should follow up with inspectors who did not submit any defects. If those inspectors didn't prepare, either they do not attend the inspection meeting or the moderator reschedules the meeting for a later date. The moderator can look for parts of the product in which many defects were found, as well as for unusually clean portions that might contain subtle defects that no one spotted. Some groups have the moderator collate the items from the inspectors' personal issue logs to provide the author with a single set of items from preparation. These approaches shift some of the burden from the author to the moderator; you'll have to judge whether your moderators have time to do this.

Conducting the Meeting

Inspection meetings are draining and stressful, even when performed professionally by experienced participants. It's hard for the author not to feel a little beaten up, no matter how valuable the experience was. The moderator can set a constructive tone by inviting every inspector to say something positive about the product at the start of the meeting.

Next, solicit global comments about the initial deliverable. If the same defect appears repeatedly, record it once and succinctly note specific occurrences as you encounter them in the product. For measurement purposes, count each instance as a separate defect, but don't discuss each of them separately. During the meeting, don't harp on issues that were already raised or rehash systemic defects that recur throughout the product. Hearing "You need more code comments" for the fifth time will try the patience of even the most receptive author.

The moderator then asks the reader to begin presenting the material to the inspection team, and you're underway.

Reading the Work Product

As described in Chapter 4, the reader presents the initial deliverable to the inspection team during the inspection meeting. Although the reader might simply read the product aloud verbatim, he typically paraphrases it one section at a time, describing the contents from a different angle or at a higher level of abstraction than you would get by reading it literally. It's rather like a teacher explaining something to a student. If the student doesn't fully understand the first explanation, expressing the concept in different words often leads to comprehension.

Describing what a dozen lines of code do is comparable to reverse-engineering the code back to the detailed design for that portion of the program. It's not the same as reviewing the design itself, because the author might not have correctly implemented the design. If the verbal design description the reader generates through his interpretation of the code doesn't match the specified design, either the implementation or the original design is wrong. This is similar to verifying a subtraction in your checkbook by adding the new balance back to the amount you subtracted to see if you get the original balance.

Each individual requirement or each element of a design model constitutes a single chunk for the reader to present as a unit. A chunk of code might contain five to ten source statements, about the size that would typically have a block comment describing it. After presenting each small chunk, the reader pauses to allow other participants to point out possible problems with that section. The moderator should try to determine that silence really means that no one has any issues, not that they are hesitant to speak up.

During preparation, the reader chooses the most effective sequence and techniques for presenting the material being inspected (Ebenau and Strauss 1994). Some portions will benefit from drawing a diagram on the whiteboard or walking through a sample execution scenario. The latter is especially valuable when inspecting requirements or test documents. In other situations, the reader could lead the team through selected test cases to ensure that everyone agrees the product would behave as expected under the test conditions (Ackerman, Buchwald, and Lewski 1989). The flow of code is easier to follow if the reader progresses down the call tree as function calls are encountered, rather than simply proceeding through the listing from beginning to end. It's hard to teach someone how to read effectively, but readers improve with practice.

Describing natural language textual items such as requirements statements in your own words can be difficult, but reading them verbatim adds no value. After all, the inspectors all read the text themselves during preparation. Paraphrasing allows someone other than the author to express his understanding of each bit of the work. If the other inspectors don't share the reader's interpretation, perhaps the group has uncovered an ambiguity, found an omission, or surfaced an assumption. If the reader has difficulty trying to describe a chunk, maybe it is too complex, poorly organized or expressed, or simply incorrect. It's appropriate for the reader to say he doesn't understand something, as this often indicates a problem.

The reader should not include too much material in a single chunk or gloss over sizeable sections of the product. I once helped inspect a requirements specification that included descriptions of two user classes for the product being specified. When the reader encountered that half-page section, he merely said, "Section 2.3 describes two classes of users, Editors and Managers," and moved on to the next section. Fortunately, the moderator intervened and asked the reader to step through the user class descriptions more thoroughly. If the moderator had not been alert, the team would not have inspected those two lengthy paragraphs, which did contain some errors.

While the reader is transmitting information, the other inspectors must be receiving and processing it effectively. Active listening can improve communication among your inspection participants, as well as in other group settings. Active listening requires that all participants be mentally engaged in the inspection meeting, combining their brainpower so that observations from the other participants stimulate thoughts that reveal new bugs. To facilitate your own effective listening, follow these guidelines:

- Eliminate physical distractions from the meeting room.
- Avoid mental and emotional distractions so you are focused on the meeting and have an open, constructive attitude.
- Come rested so you are alert and attentive.
- Control your emotions by knowing your hot buttons and thinking before you speak.
- Ask questions for clarification.
- Withhold judgment until the reader has finished presenting the key points about a section of the work product.
- Focus on the topic currently being discussed, rather than changing the subject or moving on to your own next issue.

The moderator monitors the inspection pace to see if the reader is going too rapidly or too slowly. If the reader races through the material, other inspectors might not have a chance to make comments and the team will fail to catch defects. The moderator should watch the participants' body language. A furrowed brow suggests that an inspector is confused or is contemplating making a comment. An audible intake of breath hints that someone is getting ready to speak; if the reader moves on too quickly, that contribution will be lost. Someone who suddenly begins flipping through the material might have spotted an inconsistency or be looking for a new defect similar to one that was just mentioned. If the reader progresses too slowly, the participants can become restless and bored, and the team might not cover the planned material in the allotted time. Check the body language to see if the inspectors seem to be tuning out, tapping their feet in irritation, or displaying that "come on, let's move along!" facial expression.

Raising Defects and Issues

Inspectors can point out issues and defects in several ways. Most commonly, the reader pauses briefly after presenting each section of material to permit inspectors to offer comments. The inspectors point out potential defects they found during preparation or during the meeting, and the team agrees on whether or not each is an actual defect. If you're not sure something really is a defect, log it to avoid losing the thought and let the author evaluate it later.

An alternative is to use a round-robin approach, asking each inspector in turn for his observations after the reader has presented each section. The reader moves on when all inspectors decline to present further comments. This technique is slower than simply eliciting contributions from those who have something to say when the reader pauses. It also puts pressure on individuals to come up with some input when their turns roll around. However, it does help to engage all participants in the discussion. If you try the round-robin method, use the first round to let every inspector say something positive about the work product.

Inspectors should phrase their comments thoughtfully to avoid giving offense and keep the inspection on a constructive plane. You could present an observation in the form of a question ("Are we sure that another component doesn't already provide that service?"), or you might identify a point of confusion ("I didn't see where this memory block was deallocated"). Direct your comments to the work product ("This specification is missing Section 3.5 from the template"), not to the author ("You left out Section 3.5"). Avoid comments that could sound accusatory to the author ("Did you ask the account managers if they really needed this feature?"). Authors who feel they are being beaten up in the meeting might boycott inspections of their deliverables, which negates much of the inspection's value to the author.

While I was receiving written review comments on a draft chapter of this book, one reviewer expressed a concern by saying, "How in the world have you managed to" miss some point he thought was important. Then he added, "Good grief, Karl." I respect this reviewer's experience and value his insights, but perhaps he could have phrased that bit of feedback more thoughtfully. Expressing incredulity at the author's lack of understanding does not make the author receptive to a reviewer's suggestion. A reviewer might let an inappropriate comment slip out during a discussion (oops!), but it's inexcusable in written feedback.

Inspectors don't always agree on what constitutes a defect, particularly when inspecting work products other than code. Comments on small issues that don't really affect the quality of the product can be annoying to the author. The team might question the value of inspections if only minor issues come up. When inspecting supporting project documents, look for serious problems such as missing information, ambiguous writing, incorrect assumptions, unrealistic commitments, and overlooked tasks.

Every software developer is convinced that his programming style is the best; otherwise, he would write his code differently. Therefore, raise style issues only if they interfere with understandability or maintainability or if they violate established standards. I have learned many good coding techniques by reviewing other programmers' work, so collect the best of what you observe during peer reviews to tune up your own development approaches. It's appropriate to suggest better ways to express a bit of code or to point out the risks of taking certain approaches. Do not log these as defects, though. A focus on style can distract the team from actual defects. One inspection team spent considerable time arguing about whether five lines of code should be put into a separate function. The more significant fact that the code didn't work correctly didn't get mentioned until the end of the meeting.

It is not necessary to count how many defects each inspector finds. Inspection is a team effort, and the important outcome is for the team to help the author improve the product. Your project team doesn't need metrics data to distinguish the people who do the most helpful job during inspections from those who add little value. One inspector might point out dozens of minor problems, while another brings up only the potential showstoppers; each is making an important contribution.

Recording Defects and Issues

The recorder has the challenging job of summarizing the essence of the issues discussed during the inspection meeting in a concise and inoffensive way. Recording is hard on the hand, so some moderators rotate the recorder role among several inspectors during the meeting. The moderator should make sure the recorder is keeping up with the discussion and is also able to participate. If the recorder has to ask the team to pause frequently while he captures an item, the reader is moving too quickly or too many issues are being discussed concurrently. The moderator, reader, and recorder must stay attuned to each other to maintain an appropriate pace.

The recorder uses a standard issue log (see Figure 7–4) to capture and classify each defect and issue. The moderator provides clear direction as to what items of discussion are to be logged. If inspectors found additional defects during

Issue Log

Project: ______________

Inspection ID: ______________

Inspection Date: ______________

Recorder: ______________

Origin:	**R**equirements, **D**esign, **I**mplementation, **T**esting
Type:	**M**issing, **W**rong, **E**xtra, **U**sability, **P**erformance, **Q**uestion, **S**tyle, **C**larification
Severity:	**M**ajor, minor

Defects Found: _____ **Major** _____ **Minor** **Defects Corrected:** _____ **Major** _____ **Minor**

	Origin	Type	Severity	Location	Description
1.	_____	_____	_____	_____	______________
2.	_____	_____	_____	_____	______________
3.	_____	_____	_____	_____	______________
4.	_____	_____	_____	_____	______________
5.	_____	_____	_____	_____	______________

Figure 7–4. Issue log

individual preparation that are not brought up during the meeting, the recorder should add those to the log after the meeting so that all items are collected in one place. Each entry should note the location in the work product where the issue is found (which is why it's a good idea to print line numbers on the documents being examined) and concisely describe the problem. The recorder echoes what he has written aloud to the team to verify that he noted the issue accurately and in sufficient detail for the author's subsequent rework.

As an alternative, the recorder could use an electronic tool to capture the issues, projecting the display on a large screen so all participants can see what he wrote. While completing an online defect entry form in real time might slow the meeting down, it saves transcription time if you plan to enter the defects into a database anyway. Certain groupware tools can alleviate the need for a recorder, thereby making inspections more efficient (Genuchten et al. 2001).

The issue log in Figure 7–4 contains additional spaces to record the origin, type, and severity of each defect. If this classification takes too long and slows down the inspection meeting, the recorder, author, and moderator could perform the classification after the meeting.

Origin indicates the life cycle activity during which the defect was initially injected into the work product. The choices are requirements, design, implementation, or testing, although of course you may add other categories. You can use these origin classifications regardless of what software development life-cycle your project is following. Ideally, you will detect defects in the same phase in which they are created. If many defects originated in an earlier phase, you need to improve your quality filters to catch defects closer to their origin. Some issues raised might reveal defects in earlier documents that are already baselined. Process such defects through your project's change-control procedure.

Type indicates what kind of issue or defect each item is. You can start with a simple classification scheme such as the following (Wiegers 1996a):

- Defects include items that are *missing* from the initial deliverable, things that are *wrong* (such as faulty logic, incorrect calculations, or requirements inconsistencies), and *extra* (unnecessary) elements, as well as factors that adversely affect *usability* or *performance.*
- Issues include *questions, style* suggestions other than standards violations (which are defects), and places where *clarification* is needed. Some organizations do not distinguish issues from defects, instead using defect categories such as "unclear" for items I consider to be issues.

As your organization becomes more serious about analyzing defect patterns for process improvement and defect prevention, you will need a more sophisticated defect classification method. Some possibilities include Boris Beizer's extensive "taxonomy of bugs" (1990), Hewlett-Packard's hierarchical defect classification method (Grady 1992), IBM's orthogonal defect classification (Chillarege et al. 1992; Bridge and Miller 1998), and the scheme described in IEEE Std 1044.1-1995, "Guide to Classification for Software Anomalies" (IEEE 1999c). Modify your initial defect categories to reflect the kinds of defects your own inspections reveal. If you are using rule sets or defect checklists to help discover defects, you could add another classification column to capture the specific rule or checklist item that each defect violates.

Note the *severity* of each defect (not issue) in the third column. If your project already rates the relative severity of defects found in testing or reported by customers, use that same scale for inspection defects. Many organizations use a four-level severity scale, as shown in Table 7–1 (C. Jones 1997). Usually, though, a simple grouping into major (severities 1 and 2 from Table 7–1) and minor (severities 3 and 4) defects will suffice.

Major defects are those that could have a large downstream impact and cause wasted time through rework or customer problems. They include inconsistencies between the work product and its source documents, as well as conditions that could cause a run-time failure or yield incorrect results. Plan to repair all majors, because fixing them saves the project time and money. Minor defects include cosmetic problems such as incorrectly spelled text, functionality or usability problems for which a workaround exists, and inefficient code in parts of the program that are not performance-critical. The inspection team needs judgment and experience, which will come with practice, to classify defects consistently.

The big payoff from inspection comes from finding major defects. If you aren't sure how to classify a specific defect, label it as major to ensure that the

Table 7–1: Four-level Defect Severity Scale

Severity	Meaning
1	Total application failure
2	Major function failure
3	Minor problem
4	Cosmetic problem that does not affect operation

author takes a close look at it. The numbers of major and minor defects found and corrected in each inspection go into your organization's inspection database.

Watching for Problems

The moderator stays alert for any inappropriate or ineffective behavior, which he must correct promptly lest it interfere with the team's effectiveness. The other inspectors need to respect the moderator's authority to keep the inspection meeting focused on its objectives. Consider developing a list of rules of conduct for effective inspection meetings. Watch out for the following common inspection meeting problems; Freedman and Weinberg (1990) provide suggestions for dealing with many of them.

- People arriving late for the meeting or leaving early
- Participants debating points, rather than noting key issues and moving on
- Defensiveness, rationalization, or excessive explanation by the author
- The reader describing the material in inappropriately sized chunks
- Sarcastic, provocative, or personal comments directed toward the author or other participants
- Side conversations taking place that interfere with the principal discussion
- Distracting comments from observers
- Excessive joking around that wastes time (although good-natured bantering can contribute to a comfortable session among respected colleagues)
- Lengthy discussions of style (although violations of group style or format standards are legitimate defects)
- Individuals who dominate the discussion and preclude others from contributing
- Finding only minor, superficial, or cosmetic defects and style issues

If the moderator sees that some inspectors are not contributing to the discussion, he should ensure that they have an opportunity to do so. I know of a group that invited test engineers to inspect requirements specifications, but they rarely said anything. This was unfortunate, because studying any work product from the tester's perspective is certain to reveal errors, ambiguities, and omissions. Inspectors might be reluctant to speak out if they aren't sure whether something they saw is really a defect, if the author intimidates them, or if they're shy, inexperienced, or untrained in the inspection process. Perhaps they didn't find many defects or other participants more quickly raised the defects they did spot.

People are sometimes reluctant to offer their opinions publicly for fear of revealing their own ignorance. The moderator needs to create a safe environment where everyone feels free to make comments, knowing they'll be taken in a constructive spirit and won't be held against the speaker. If certain individuals are not participating, the moderator should interrupt the meeting and say, "We seem to have an imbalance in participation. Why do you think that is?" The ensuing discussion might provide understanding that encourages the silent team members to contribute.

I once worked with a very shy software developer whose opinions I valued highly. Although Annette wouldn't speak up spontaneously in a meeting, she would respond to questions I asked her in a way that stressed her expertise and perspective. The moderator should work with reticent inspectors to understand their point of view and ensure that they are preparing adequately and understand the inspection process. It can help if the moderator explains why everyone's contributions are valuable.

It's easy for an inspection team to become sidetracked by the stimulation of solving interesting technical problems:

"Does anyone have any problems with requirement 4.7.3?" asked Jason, the moderator.

Margie said, "I have a question. The requirement says that the system measures the tank temperature every 10 seconds for 1000 seconds and then calculates and stores the equilibrium temperature. But it doesn't say what the system is supposed to do if the tank hasn't reached thermal stability after 1000 seconds. It looks like a missing exception to me."

"You're right!" exclaimed the requirements specification's author, Frank. "This assumes that the tank reaches thermal stability after 1000 seconds, but it might not. Maybe we should change the measurement period to 1500 seconds."

Dimitri, the recorder, protested, "That would be too long for most situations. If it hasn't stabilized after 1000 seconds, it probably isn't going to. The system should abort the run, display an error message, and write a descriptive record to the log file."

Jason broke in. "Okay, it looks like Margie spotted a missing exception. We can't resolve this here today. Frank, can you please ask the customer what the system should do if the temperature hasn't stabilized after 1000 seconds? It's too bad he turned down our invitation to this inspection. Dimitri, did you get the problem recorded okay?"

"Yes," replied Dimitri. "In requirement 4.7.3, the system's behavior if the temperature hasn't stabilized after 1000 seconds is not defined."

"Thank you," said Jason. "Is there anything else on 4.7.3?" Everyone shook his head. "Okay, let's move on."

Don't spend more than about one minute deciding how to fix a defect during the meeting, because time spent talking about a problem is time not spent finding more problems. If an inspector has ideas about how best to address a particular defect, he and the author can put their heads together during the rework stage. Have the recorder note the individuals with whom the author should work on specific issues. Similarly, spend only a minute or so discussing whether an issue really is a defect. If the team cannot agree in that time, record it as a defect and move on.

If the problem-solving continues past a minute or so, the moderator should ensure that the recorder has noted the issue and guide the group back to the central goal of logging defects. The moderator needs to use his judgment, rather than using a stopwatch to enforce dogmatic conformance to the one-minute rule. If it appears that a discussion will lead to deeper understanding that might reveal some additional defects, the moderator should let the discussion progress until it no longer seems constructive (Doolan 1992).

Occasionally you might encounter a situation where a problem raised is a showstopper—the inspection (and perhaps the project) cannot continue until some fundamental problem is resolved. On another occasion, the moderator might judge that the number and severity of defects being reported indicate that the product really is not ready for inspection or needs to be rebuilt. Then it's appropriate to suspend the inspection and perhaps to switch into problem-solving mode. Mark the appraisal as "Inspection Not Completed" on the inspection summary report and state why. Don't pretend that you actually finished the inspection if you converted the meeting into a brainstorming session.

The moderator should also notice if the meeting has moved into making inappropriate decisions—as opposed to observations—about the work product, its requirements, or other project issues. For example, when no customer representative is present during a requirements specification inspection, developers sometimes choose to include certain functionality on their own authority. The inspection team isn't the right group of people to make certain decisions about the product or project. Sometimes issues will arise that require someone other than the author to take follow-up action after the meeting. The moderator records these action items on a separate sheet of paper and delivers them to the appropriate individuals for resolution. If these action items pertain to the work product being inspected, the moderator should confirm that they have been resolved before declaring the inspection complete during the follow-up stage.

When I observe a group performing a practice inspection during a training class, sometimes I can't even tell who is supposed to be moderating. It's easy for the moderator himself to get caught up in problem-solving discussions or other diversions. A moderator who fails to control the meeting isn't doing an effective job. If the moderator does go down an unproductive path, any other inspector should feel free to bring the discussion back on track.

Product Appraisal

At the end of the inspection meeting (or the final meeting, if multiple meetings were needed), the participants agree on an appraisal—sometimes called the disposition—that determines the future fate of the initial deliverable (Ebenau and Strauss 1994; Freedman and Weinberg 1990). This appraisal represents the team's conclusion about whether the work product is correct and complete. Possible appraisals are:

- *Accepted as is.* Some minor corrections may be necessary, but the follow-up stage can be omitted.
- *Accepted conditionally.* Minor revision is needed, followed by verification.
- *Reinspect following rework.* Major restructuring is required, many defects must be corrected, more than a specified fraction of the product must be revised, too few errors were found during preparation, or the inspection data was out of line with your process averages for that type of work product. The team wants to take another look before declaring the product to have passed the inspection. All inspectors should receive a copy of the issue log, indicating which items were resolved and how, along with the reworked deliverable for preparation. The reinspection might concentrate on just selected portions or aspects of the deliverable.
- *Inspection not completed.* You didn't cover all the planned material during the meeting. A second meeting, perhaps with just a subset of the inspection team, is needed to complete the inspection. Or, the inspection was abandoned for some reason.

The team should agree in advance on how they will determine the product appraisal by selecting an appropriate rule that governs their decision-making process (Gottesdiener 2001). Possible decision rules include a majority vote, consensus, unanimity (which is not the same as consensus), or having the moderator make the call. Gilb (1998) strongly advises against voting, recommending instead that objective evaluations of the likely number of remaining defects per page be used to decide whether the initial deliverable passed the inspection. Until you accumulate sufficient historical data, however, you can't make such quantitative evaluations. Designating a single individual to determine the appraisal is not the best approach, either. Asking one person to decide undermines the principle of having the inspection team share responsibility for the outcome. Ideally, the team will reach a consensus on the final appraisal. The moderator should poll the participants to see how strongly they agree with the outcome.

If the inspectors cannot all agree on the same appraisal, go with the most conservative opinion expressed by any inspector (Freedman and Weinberg 1990). For example, if most participants recommend accepting conditionally, while one inspector insists that the product should be reinspected following rework, the appraisal should be "reinspect following rework." Some inspectors might resist this philosophy, protesting that the majority should rule. However, rejecting the most conservative opinion destroys the incentive for people with strong minority opinions to speak their minds. Remember, the objective of the inspection is not to provide a seal of approval but to find places where the product needs improvement.

Management must respect the inspection team's appraisal. If management rejects the team's recommendation to reinspect or rebuild a badly flawed product, this can undermine the entire inspection program. Why participate if your professional opinion is rejected because it's not what management wanted to hear?

Closing the Meeting

After the team determines the product appraisal, the moderator brings the meeting to a close and completes the inspection summary report. For an appraisal of "accepted conditionally," the group decides who will verify the author's rework. Often the moderator handles follow-up, although he could ask a quality engineer or another inspector with the right specialized knowledge to evaluate the author's changes.

Whether you have the participants sign the inspection summary report is a cultural preference. A signature indicates that the signer agrees with the outcome of the inspection, showing group commitment to the quality of both the work product and the inspection itself (Freedman and Weinberg 1990). If an inspector is reluctant to sign, find out why. He might have reservations about the product that he didn't bring up during the discussion, might object to the way the inspection was handled, or might have some other unstated opinion the moderator should know about.

The moderator provides copies of the completed issue log to the author and the verifier. The issue log is not to be shared beyond the inspection team unless the author chooses to do so. David Gelperin points out that technical peer reviews serve practitioners first and managers second (SQE 1995b). Managers are entitled to know about the review process that was used, who participated, and their conclusions about the work product. However, they aren't entitled to know exactly how many bugs of each type were discovered in a specific author's deliverable. Managers, process engineers, and other project team members may view summaries of data from multiple inspections but not individual issue logs. The peer review coordinator may see the issue log if he needs to enter detailed defect data into the inspection database.

Improving the Inspection Process

In the spirit of process improvement, the moderator concludes the inspection meeting by collecting comments from the participants on this inspection experience and how it could be improved. Figure 7–5 contains an inspection *Lessons Learned questionnaire* with several such self-reflecting questions. Possible inspection improvements are to add an item to a defect checklist, change the recommended preparation or inspection rates based on accumulated rate and defect data, or modify the project roles that should inspect a specific type of work product. Some participants may prefer to provide their comments to the moderator privately, particularly if interpersonal issues are involved.

Tracking selected metrics provides another way to look for areas of improvement in your inspection process. For example, one company noticed that the chart of open inspection issues had an upward trend, indicating that the inspections weren't fully reaching closure. They changed their process to make moderators responsible for closing each meeting's open issues. Spending a few moments to look for ways to make the next inspection even more effective is a small investment in continuous process improvement.

Inspection Lessons Learned Questionnaire

1. Did the inspection meet the author's and team's objectives? If not, why not?
2. Does the team feel they were able to significantly improve the quality of the work product through the inspection?
3. Did everyone have sufficient time to do preparation? If not, how much time do they need prior to the inspection meeting?
4. Did anyone use the checklist or rules for this type of work product during preparation? Was it helpful in finding defects? If not, why not? Can the checklist or rules be improved?
5. Were the right participants present? If not, who was missing or didn't need to be there?
6. Were the inspection entry and exit criteria followed correctly?
7. How could the meeting be run better?
8. Does anyone need help in being able to participate effectively in inspections?
9. Are there any other suggestions for improving the inspection process?

Figure 7–5. Inspection Lessons Learned questionnaire

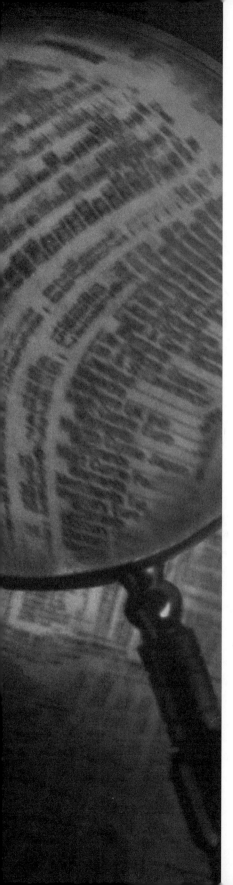

CHAPTER EIGHT

Bringing Closure

A n inspection isn't finished when the author walks out of the inspection meeting with an issue log. Work is required to correct errors and make other improvements in the initial deliverable. Afterward, someone might need to verify that the author's rework was performed correctly. A final inspection activity analyzes the defects that the inspection team discovered to improve the organization's development and quality practices. This chapter describes the rework, follow-up, and causal analysis inspection stages.

The Rework Stage

Nearly every inspection identifies some defects that should be corrected and suggests improvements that the author may or may not choose to implement. The inspection process includes rework as an explicit inspection stage (see Figure 8–1). The author should complete rework promptly so he can baseline the corrected deliverable and move on to his next project task. Note that if extensive rework is needed, the product might not have been ready for inspection; perhaps a peer deskcheck would have revealed this with a small amount of effort.

The author must address every issue on the inspection issue log and the typo lists received from the inspectors. If your goal is to deliver defect-free software, the author needs to correct every known error. Defects that the inspection team agreed were of major severity are prime candidates for

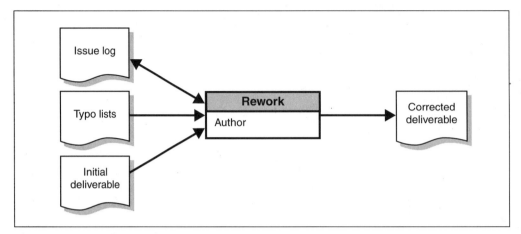

Figure 8–1. The inspection rework stage

repair, because those are the ones that can have serious consequences. Defects found in deliverables from the early life-cycle stages should always be corrected because their impact is amplified so greatly as time goes by. The decision to correct minor defects and typos is usually up to the author, with input from his team members or management. However, if authors persistently decline to make such changes, inspectors might begin classifying every defect as "major" just to get the author to take them seriously.

Some projects choose to leave known defects uncorrected, perhaps to meet tight delivery schedules or because they expect the remaining bugs to have only a small impact on the customer. Be careful that the team does not make short-sighted decisions that lead to shipping a product that meets with poor customer satisfaction, generates unfavorable published product reviews, or incurs high maintenance costs. If the author isn't certain what to do, he should consult with the project's quality engineer or with other colleagues who can help identify the defects that must be fixed.

If the author elects not to make certain corrections, he should note the rationale behind those decisions on the issue log and enter those bugs in the project's defect-tracking system. (If your project doesn't have a defect-tracking system, make that a top priority for your process improvement program.) That way the bugs won't come as a surprise when someone rediscovers them during system testing or in operation. These records will also remind major stakeholders that they made explicit tradeoff decisions during the product's development. If appropriate, you may defer certain defects to be corrected in subsequent product releases.

During the rework stage, the author also addresses issues other than defects that were raised. Inspectors might have brought up questions that need to be explored and answered. They might have flagged sections of the initial deliverable as needing clarification or having style problems. Upon exploration, the author sometimes discovers that an issue that was raised as a simple question is in fact a defect. Other logged defects might turn out to be correct after all. The author reclassifies such items during follow-up, corrects the issue log, and reflects the changes in the defect metrics that he reports to the moderator. The inspection team should have access to the final issue log to see whether any items were reclassified and to learn which defects were not corrected.

The Follow-Up Stage

An important part of executing any process is to verify that the process steps were performed correctly. The follow-up stage, illustrated in Figure 8–2, fulfills this function for an inspection, getting help from another pair of eyes to ensure that rework was done properly. The verifier could be the moderator, a quality engineer, or another inspector to whom the moderator delegated the verification task. The product of follow-up is a baselined deliverable, considerably improved from the original, that provides a solid foundation for the subsequent development work.

One purpose of follow-up is to verify that the author resolved all open issues from the inspection meeting appropriately and made reasonable decisions as to

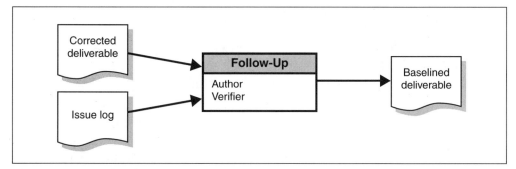

Figure 8–2. The inspection follow-up stage

which defects (if any) to leave uncorrected. Tracking inspection issues to closure is a characteristic of a mature inspection process. If inspectors see that authors do not correct many of the defects found through inspection, their motivation to participate in future inspections diminishes. On the other hand, if the author attempts to accommodate everybody's ideas, he can be frustrated by the rework time needed. The follow-up stage provides a mechanism for balancing the author's judgment about the changes to make against the verifier's perspective of adequate product quality.

A second objective of follow-up is to determine that the changes made in the initial deliverable were made correctly, without introducing secondary defects. Follow-up can help avoid the problem of bad fixes, in which either the original error was not properly corrected or the changes that were made broke some other part of the system. Approximately one in twenty defect corrections in fairly simple code introduces a secondary error. This risk can soar to 60 percent in complex modules that contain extensive branching logic (C. Jones 1996). Bad fixes are especially common when you're hastily making a one-line change, a change that seems so straightforward that verification is not needed.

I once experienced a streak of bad fixes when I was correcting several small bugs that users reported in some software I had written. The underlying cause was haste. I was in such a rush to make the changes and install the modified code that I skimped on testing and didn't ask any of my colleagues to check my work. The embarrassment of repeatedly declaring bugs to be fixed, only to be informed that they really weren't, made me change my approach to this type of small mainte-nance action. My bad fix problem went away when I began taking my time, testing more carefully, and benefiting from quick peer reviews.

The appraisal that the inspection team issues at the close of the inspection meeting determines the appropriate follow-up activity. If the appraisal was to accept the product as is, the follow-up step is waived. The team trusts the author to make whatever minor corrections he feels are appropriate. If the product was accepted conditionally, the moderator or someone else checks the changes made during rework.

If a product requires major modification, the appraisal should indicate that a partial or complete reinspection is needed following rework. A subgroup of the original inspection team could perform the verification, or the entire team could examine the modified product in a second full inspection. Because performing a second inspection is costly, the team should think carefully about requiring that form of follow-up verification. Reinspecting early-stage deliverables, such as requirements specifications, will do the most good. As with most software quality decisions, you need to balance the risk of having serious defects remain un-detected against the cost of looking for those defects.

When the author and the verifier agree that rework is complete, the author provides the moderator with final counts for the numbers of major and minor defects found, the number of each that he corrected, and the total labor hours spent performing rework and follow-up. The rework effort could include time spent by individuals besides the author and the verifier. The defect counts go on the issue log, and the moderator notes the actual rework effort on the inspection summary report. The moderator delivers all of these metrics to the project's peer review coordinator, who enters them into the inspection database. Your organi-zation can use this accumulated data to estimate the effort needed for future inspections and to judge inspection efficiency and effectiveness, as described in Chapter 9.

The Causal Analysis Stage

Studying the patterns of defects found in different kinds of work products and understanding their causes are powerful tools for process improvement and defect prevention. Performing the causal analysis stage illustrated in Figure 8–3 is a way to heed George Santayana's warning that "Those who cannot remember the past are condemned to repeat it." Defect causal analysis enables organizational learning that can lead to consistently superior products, just as project retrospectives improve your ability to execute complex software projects (Kerth 2001).

A simple causal analysis action is to tally how many defects arise from each identified root cause. Such a Pareto analysis reveals the underlying causes that lead to most of the problems. The familiar 80/20 rule suggests that about 80 per-cent of the defects can usually be traced to just 20 percent of the various under-lying causes. Correcting that vital 20 percent of root causes provides the greatest

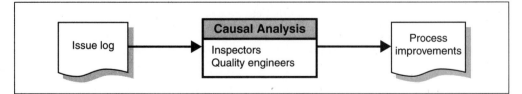

Figure 8–3. The inspection causal analysis stage

immediate quality improvement. C. L. Jones (1985) described a more sophisticated defect causal analysis process in detail.

The Space Shuttle Onboard Software project provides an excellent example of defect causal analysis (Paulk et al. 1995). The project team followed a four-stage process:

1. Determine the cause of each defect found and correct the defect.
2. Correct the aspect of the development process that led to introduction of the defect to reduce the chance of making similar errors in the future.
3. Correct the quality processes from which the defect had escaped to improve the team's ability to catch similar defects earlier in the life cycle. Such changes could lead to better testing methods, a revised inspection process, or improved analysis techniques.
4. Examine the entire product for similar defects that might remain unnoticed.

Some organizations perform causal analysis during a so-called "third hour" of discussion that follows the typical two-hour inspection meeting, although of course you could hold such a meeting at any later time (NASA 1993). The participants in this third-hour meeting might include several of the inspectors, quality engineers, outside technical experts, and selected managers who are participating from a technical point of view.

Another type of analysis studies trends and statistics on the discovered defects to determine improvement actions the organization should take. Defect classification and analysis is a way to "know your enemy." You can be most successful in the battle against bugs if you know what kinds of bugs you're up against, where they live, and how to kill them. Grouping the defects found by inspection according to type (or category) and frequency of occurrence reveals patterns that lead to ideas for changing your development processes to reduce such errors in the future. This defect prevention is the long-term strategic benefit of inspection, with a leveraging effect far greater than that of removing defects through inspection of individual work products. For example, one IS organization found that it could attribute many of its software defects to requirements errors. In response, they improved their requirements elicitation practices and performed more prototyping, which reduced their requirements errors.

Today's software developer has many defect removal techniques available, including deskchecking, compilation, static and dynamic code analysis, testing, test coverage measurement, and peer review. Developers who study their personal defect data to see which techniques work best for them can modify their personal software process to use those removal methods routinely (Humphrey 1995). Inspection data can also indicate ways to improve the inspection process itself. If certain types of errors made in one development phase, such as ambiguous requirements, are being caught in subsequent phases, devise methods to catch those errors closer to their point of origin.

Inspection Exit Criteria

The exit criteria for a process puts forward the conditions that must be satisfied to declare that an execution of the process was successfully completed. An inspection is completed when the exit criteria for that entire inspection are satisfied. The moderator assesses whether the inspection's exit criteria have been met when he meets with the author during follow-up. Possible qualitative exit criteria include the following:

❑ The author's or team's inspection objectives were achieved.

❑ All open issues were tracked to closure.

❑ All major defects were corrected.

❑ Any uncorrected minor defects were logged into the project's defect-tracking system, with the verifier's concurrence.

❑ If changes were made in a previously completed component, it passed all regression tests.

After the exit criteria have been satisfied, the author baselines the corrected deliverable and checks it into the project's configuration management system. The inspection is now complete!

As you accumulate data from multiple inspections, your team will become able to define quantitative exit criteria. Chapter 9 discusses ways to analyze inspection data by using statistical process control techniques. You can define control limits for preparation and inspection rates, defect densities, and other parameters based on your historical experience. When you reach this point of stability in your inspections and your development processes, you can predict approximately how much material you can inspect per hour and how many defects you are likely to find. An inspection whose parameters fall outside the statistically expected ranges will not satisfy its exit criteria. Reinspection might be needed to reach an acceptable level of confidence in the product's quality.

When you declare that a work product has passed an inspection, you're saying that the likely number of remaining defects is low enough to continue development work based on that deliverable. Simply finding a lot of defects should not give you confidence that you have found them all. Until you know how effectively your inspections remove defects from different kinds of work products, you can't make any confident or quantitative statements about the probable remaining defect density. Strive to accumulate and analyze data from multiple inspections so you can make a serious judgment as to whether each product is clean enough to satisfy its inspection exit criteria.

CHAPTER NINE

Analyzing Inspection Data

My friend Nick is a quality manager at a company that is respected for its superior software development and quality practices. Nick once told me, "We only found two major defects in our latest code inspection, but we expected to find between four and six. We're trying to figure out what's going on. Did we miss some, or was this code particularly clean for some reason?"

Few organizations can make such precise statements about the quality of their software products. Nick's organization has stable, repeatable development processes in place and has accumulated inspection data for several years. Analyzing historical data lets Nick predict the likely defect density in a given deliverable. When a specific inspection's results depart significantly from the norm, Nick can ask probing questions to understand why. Did the inspectors prepare at the optimum rate? Did they use suitable analysis techniques? Were they adequately trained and experienced in inspection? Was the author more or less experienced than average? Was the product more or less complex than average? You can't reach this depth of understanding without data.

Why Collect Data?

The recording of data about the review process and product quality is a distinguishing characteristic of formal peer reviews. For simplicity I will use the term "inspection" in this discussion, although these measurement concepts apply to any type of formal review. Data answers important questions, provides quantifiable insights and historical perspective, and lets you base decisions on facts instead of perceptions or memories. For example, one organization learned that it could inspect requirements specifications written by experienced analysts twice as fast as those written by novices because they contained fewer defects. This data revealed the need to train and mentor novice analysts. Another organization improved its development process by studying data on defect injection rates and the types of defects their inspections did not catch (Bianco 1996). This example illustrates the importance of recording the life-cycle phases during which each defect is created and discovered.

One way to choose appropriate metrics is the Goal-Question-Metric, or GQM, technique (Basili and Rombach 1988). First, state your business or technical *goals*. Next, identify *questions* you need to answer to tell if you are reaching those goals. Finally, select *metrics* that will let you answer those questions. One goal might be to reduce your rework costs through inspection. Answers to the following questions could help you judge whether you are reaching that worthy goal:

- What percentage of each project's development effort is spent on rework?
- How much effort do our inspections consume? How much do they save?
- How many defects do we discover by inspection? What kind? How severe? At what life-cycle stage?
- What percentage of the defects in our products do our inspections remove?
- Do we spend less time testing, debugging, and maintaining products that we inspected than those we did not?

Figure 9–1 shows a progression of benefits that inspection measurements can provide. The individual data items you begin collecting don't tell you much by themselves. Tracking some metrics calculated from those data items reveals averages and trends of your team's preparation and inspection rates, defect densities, inspection effectiveness, and other factors. These trends help you detect anomalous inspection results, provided that your development and inspection processes are consistent. They also help you estimate how many additional defects you can expect to find in the remaining life-cycle phases or through customer usage. Correlations between pairs of metrics help you understand, say, how increasing the preparation rate affects inspection efficiency. For the maximum rewards, use defect causal analysis and statistical process control to guide improvements in your development processes and quality management methods.

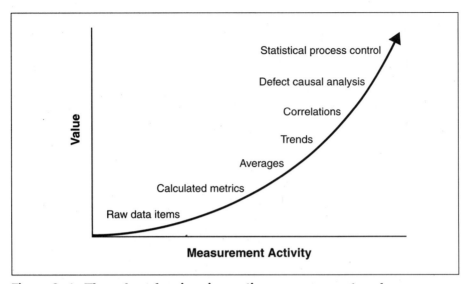

Figure 9–1. The value of various inspection measurement analyses

Don't make your measurement process so elaborate that it inhibits the inspections themselves. Establishing a peer review culture and finding bugs is more important than meticulously recording masses of data. One of my groups routinely conducted various types of peer reviews, recorded basic data items, and tracked several metrics (Wiegers 1996a). We retained our issue logs with the intention of storing the defect information in a database, although we never got around to that step. Nonetheless, the entire team recognized the value we obtained from the reviews and they became an ingrained element of our software engineering culture.

Some Measurement Caveats

Software measurement is a sensitive subject. It's important to be honest and nonjudgmental about metrics. Data is neither good nor bad, so a manager must neither reward nor punish anyone for his metrics results. The first time a practitioner is punished for some data he reported is the last time the manager will get accurate data. Word of such misuse of the data spreads quickly among the other team members. Defects found prior to inspection should remain private to the author, while information about defects found in a specific inspection can be shared only with the project team, not with its managers (Grady 1992). Aggregate the data from multiple inspections to monitor averages and trends in your inspection process without compromising the privacy of individual authors. The project manager should share aggregated inspection data with the rest of the team so they see the insights the data can provide and recognize the inspection benefits.

Beware the phenomenon known as *measurement dysfunction* (Austin 1996). Measurement dysfunction arises when the measurement process or the ways in which managers use the data lead to counterproductive behaviors by the people providing the data (see Figure 9–2). People ordinarily behave in the ways for which they are rewarded and avoid behaviors that could have unpleasant consequences. Some forms of measurement dysfunction that can arise from peer reviews are defect severity inflation or deflation, artificial defect closure, and distorted defect densities, preparation times, and defect discovery rates (P. Johnson 1996b).

There is a natural tension between the author's desire to create defect-free products and the inspectors' desire to find lots of bugs. Evaluating either authors or inspectors according to the number of defects found during an inspection will lead to conflict. If you rate inspectors based on how many defects they find, they'll report many defects, even if it means arguing with the author about whether every small issue truly is a defect. It's not necessary to know who identified each defect or to count how many each inspector found. What is important is that all team members participate constructively in reviews. Keep your data collection objective and impersonal, and make sure managers avoid the temptation to misuse the data for individual performance evaluation by not making individual defect data available to them.

Figure 9–2. Dysfunctional measurement in action. (DILBERT© UFS. Reprinted by permission.)

It's tempting to overanalyze the inspection data. Avoid trying to draw conclusions from data collected shortly after launching your peer review program. If you begin tracking a new metric, give it time to stabilize and make sure you're getting reliable data before jumping to any conclusions. The trends you observe are more significant than any single data point.

Basic Data Items and Metrics

Software teams should collect data because it lets them answer questions that currently available information does not, not just because the data seems interesting or is easy to count. The basic dimensions of software measurement are size, time, effort, and quality. Although you could measure dozens of inspection data items in these categories, the data items listed in Table 9–1 will give you a solid start on inspection measurement. The inspection summary report illustrated in Figure 7–3 and the issue log from Figure 7–4 contain spaces to record all these data items. Whenever possible, use tools to count objects such as lines of code consistently, according to your organization's conventions (for example, nonblank, noncomment physical source statements). If you don't have code-counting conventions, this is a good opportunity to define some.

As you gain experience, you might elect to subdivide some of these data items. You could separate rework effort from follow-up effort; distinguish inspections of new, modified, and reused code; or separate the metrics for major and minor defects. Increase the measurement complexity only when you have specific questions that require more detailed data. I recommend you begin by collecting all the items listed in Table 9–1. The effort needed to capture and store this information is small, but it is impossible to reconstruct the data if you decide later that you want it.

You can calculate several metrics from the data items in Table 9–1 that will give you insight into your inspection process (Gilb and Graham 1993; Barnard and Price 1994; Harding 1998). Table 9–2 describes several inspection metrics and shows how to calculate them from the basic data items.

The Inspection Database

You will need a repository in which to store your inspection data, along with query, reporting, and charting tools to monitor averages and trends in the metrics for a series of inspections. To get started quickly, use the spreadsheet available

Table 9–1. Some Basic Inspection Data Items

Category	Data Item	Description
Size	Size.Planned	Lines of code or document pages that you planned to inspect.
	Size.Actual	Lines of code or document pages that were actually inspected.
Time	Time.Meeting	Duration of the inspection meeting in hours; if several meetings were needed to complete the inspection, include them all in this total.
Effort	Effort.Planning	Total labor hours the moderator and author spent on planning, scheduling meetings, assembling and distributing the inspection package, and the like.
	Effort.Overview	Total labor hours spent on the overview stage (multiply the number of participants by the duration of the overview meeting, if one was held).
	Effort.Preparation	Total labor hours spent on individual preparation (sum the individual preparation times from all of the inspectors).
	Effort.Meeting	Total labor hours spent in the inspection meeting (multiply Time.Meeting by Number.of.Inspectors).
	Effort.Rework	Total labor hours the author spent correcting defects in the initial deliverable and making other improvements based on the inspection results; include verification time from the follow-up stage.
Defects	Defects.Found.Major	Number of major defects found during the inspection.

(continued)

Table 9–1. Some Basic Inspection Data Items (*cont.*)

	Defects.Found.Minor	Number of minor defects found during the inspection.
	Defects.Corrected.Major	Number of major defects corrected during rework.
	Defects.Corrected.Minor	Number of minor defects corrected during rework.
Other	Number.of.Inspectors	Number of people, not counting observers, who participated in the inspection meeting.
	Product.Appraisal	Inspection team's assessment of the inspected work product (accepted as is, accepted conditionally, reinspect following rework, inspection not completed).

from the Web site that accompanies this book. The spreadsheet is not a robust, full-featured inspection database—just a simple tool to help you begin accumulating inspection data easily.

The Inspection Data spreadsheet is implemented in Microsoft Excel. It contains three linked worksheets that accommodate the data items from Table 9–1 and the metrics from Table 9–2. The Inspection Info worksheet contains descriptive information about each inspection, the data items in the Other category, and the major calculated metrics. Enter the time and effort data items into the Effort worksheet. The defect counts in various categories go into the Defects worksheet, along with the number of defects the author corrected during rework. A Help Info worksheet contains instructions for using the spreadsheet and inserting new rows by using a macro. This approach stores the data for individual inspections

Table 9–2. Suggested Inspection Metrics

Metric	*Description*	*Formula*	*Application*
Defect.Density	Number of defects found per unit of material inspected	Defects.Found.Total / Size.Actual	Evaluate document quality; track trends to evaluate the impact of defect prevention or earlier defect detection activities; compare to the number of defects found in later life-cycle stages to judge inspection effectiveness
Defects.Corrected. Total	Sum of the number of major and minor defects corrected	Defects.Corrected.Major + Defects.Corrected.Minor	Divide by Defects.Found.Total to track the fraction of all defects found that are beingcorrected during rework; calculate average rework effort per defect
Defects.Found.Total	Sum of the number of major and minor defects found	Defects.Found.Major + Defects.Found.Minor	Evaluate effectiveness and efficiency of inspection at finding defects
Effort.Inspection	Total effort expended on the inspection	Effort.Planning + Effort.Overview + Effort.Preparation + Effort.Meeting + Effort.Rework	Calculate the total cost of inspections in either labor hours or dollars (labor hours multiplied by fully-burdened hourly employee cost); combine with estimated cost savings from defects found to estimate the return on investment from inspections

(continued)

Table 9–2. Suggested Inspection Metrics (*cont.*)

Metric	Description	Formula	Application
Effort.per.Defect	Average total labor hours expended to find a defect	(Effort.Planning + Effort.Overview + Effort.Preparation + Effort.Meeting) / Defects.Found.Total	Cost to find a defect by inspection, which you can compare with the cost to deal with a defect found later in the product's life-cycle; compare this to the effort of finding defects through testing or other means to identify the most cost-effective defect removal technique
Effort.per.Unit.Size	Average labor hours expended to inspect a unit of work product material	Effort.Inspection / Size.Actual	Estimate the cost of inspecting the work products created on a project
Percent.Inspected	Percentage of the planned material that was actually inspected	100 * Size.Actual / Size.Planned	Evaluate accuracy of inspection planning
Percent.Majors	Percentage of the total defects found that were classified as of major severity	100 * Defects.Found. Major / Defects.Found. Total	Judge whether inspections focus on finding minor or major errors
Rate.Inspection	Average quantity of material inspected per meeting hour	Size.Actual / Time.Meeting	Correlate with Effort.per.Defect and Size.Actual to determine the optimum inspection rate for discovering the maximum number of defects; use for planning future inspection effort

(continued)

Table 9–2. Suggested Inspection Metrics (*cont.*)

Metric	*Description*	*Formula*	*Application*
Rate.Preparation	Average quantity of material covered per labor hour of individual preparation; assumes that all material planned for inspection was examined	Size.Planned / (Effort.Preparation / Number.of.Inspectors)	Correlate with Effort.per.Defect and Size.Planned to determine the optimum preparation rate for discovering the maximum number of defects; use for planning future inspection effort
Rework.per.Defect	Average number of labor hours needed to correct and verify a defect	Effort.Rework / Defects.Corrected.Total	Compare the cost of fixing defects found by inspection with the cost of fixing them if they were found later in the product's life-cycle, to judge the benefits from inspection

in reverse chronological order, with the most recent entries at the top. You can modify the spreadsheet if, for example, you wish to focus only on major defects or to exploit the charting and statistical analysis features of Excel.

The units used for measuring work product size are different for code and for other documents. Therefore, you will need separate spreadsheets for each major type of work product being inspected: source code, requirements specifications, design documents, test cases, and so on. The Web site for this book contains one spreadsheet for code inspections, another for inspections of other documents, and a third with some sample code inspection data. In a genuine database, you can simply define the document type by an appropriate data attribute.

Data Analysis

As you accumulate data from multiple inspections of a given type of work product, the spreadsheet will calculate the averages of the metrics. You can then use scatter charts to look for correlations between pairs of metrics (Barnard and Price 1994; Ebenau 1994). The basic spreadsheet I've provided does not contain any scatter charts, but it would not be difficult to add those that you find informative.

Figure 9–3 shows a sample scatter chart. This chart plots Effort.per.Defect (the average labor hours needed to find one defect) against Rate.Preparation (the average lines of code per hour studied by an inspector during preparation) for a set of code inspections. Each data point represents a separate inspection. For example, one inspection that had a preparation rate of 100 lines per hour found one defect for every 0.5 hour of preparation time.

This chart shows that inspections having preparation rates slower than about 200 lines of code per hour are less efficient than those with higher preparation rates. That is, it takes more hours of work, on average, to find each defect if the inspectors prepare slowly. This doesn't necessarily mean that you should increase your preparation rate to boost efficiency. A plot of Defect.Density (the number of defects found per thousand lines of code) versus Rate.Preparation would show that effectiveness *decreases* with higher preparation rates. That is, the faster you go, the fewer defects you find. Figure 5–4 illustrated a similar correlation between Defect.Density and Rate.Inspection. This type of data analysis helps you judge the optimum balance between efficiency and effectiveness (Barnard and Price 1994).

As your organization establishes repeatable development, management, and inspection processes, you can use *statistical process control* (SPC) to monitor key

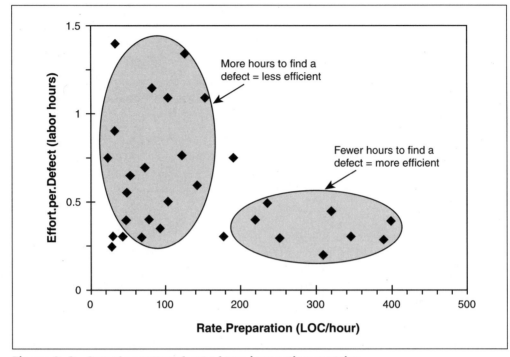

Figure 9–3. Sample scatter chart of two inspection metrics

inspection parameters. SPC is a set of analytical techniques for measuring the stability of a process and identifying when individual performances of the process fall outside the expected range of variation, or control limits. Points that lie beyond the control limits stimulate an inquiry to understand why, perhaps leading to process changes. The historical data trends from a process that is in control enable prediction of future outcomes of the process. Inspection metrics that are amenable to SPC include Rate.Preparation, Rate.Inspection, Size.Actual, and Defect.Density. The details of SPC are beyond the scope of this book, but several authors have published excellent experience reports and explanations of how to apply SPC to inspection data (Ebenau 1994; Weller 2000; Florac, Carleton, and Barnard 2000).

As a simple illustration of SPC, Figure 9–4 depicts a *control chart* containing preparation rates (lines of source code per hour) from 25 code inspections. The control chart plots specific data (Rate.Preparation) from the process being observed (inspection preparation) versus the set of observations (inspection

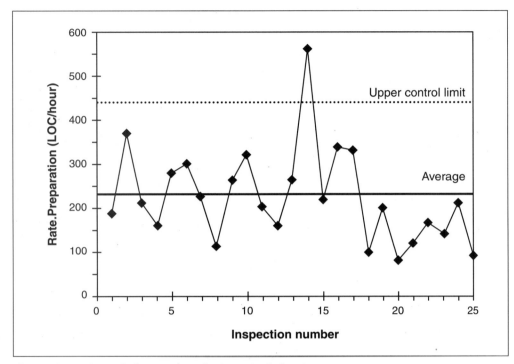

Figure 9–4. Sample inspection data control chart

number). The average preparation rate was 230 lines of code per hour, shown with the solid horizontal line. The *upper control limit,* shown as the dashed line at 440 LOC/hour, is a statistic that attempts to discriminate normal variation or noise in the process from variations that can be attributed to some assignable cause. Points that lie beyond the upper control limit indicate "out-of-control" values that warrant investigation.

Figure 9–4 shows that the preparation rate for inspection 14 was an abnormally high 560 LOC/hour, which lies beyond the upper control limit. Because inspection 14 departed from the expected preparation rate range, its results should be viewed with caution. Did inspectors cut their preparation shorter than the organization's historical data recommends for optimum defect discovery? Was there something unusual about the work product—particularly straightforward or clean code, reused code, or tested code—that led to a justifiable increase in preparation rate? Was the inspection team particularly experienced and efficient?

Correlating defect densities with preparation rates for a repeatable process lets you judge whether a code component that had an abnormally high preparation rate might suffer future quality problems because of residual defects. This is the kind of data analysis that allowed my friend Nick, the quality manager mentioned at the beginning of this chapter, to predict how many major defects he expected to find when inspecting a new code module. Statistical analysis tells you whether your inspection process is under control and provides a powerful tool for analyzing accumulated inspection data.

Inspection data can also indicate whether you are catching defects in the same life-cycle phase in which they were created. Because the cost of finding defects in subsequent stages increases so rapidly, your goal should be to achieve 100 percent *defect containment,* with no bugs escaping into downstream work products. The inspection issue log in Figure 7–4 includes the Origin field for recording the life-cycle stage at which each defect was injected into the product. Comparing these injection points with the type of work product in which the defects were found indicates your defect containment (Stutzke 1999).

Measuring the Impact of Inspections

Participants can subjectively judge the value of inspections. Sometimes, though, a more quantitative benefit analysis is desired. Ideally, you will be able to demonstrate that inspections are saving your project team, company, or customers more time than they consume. One aspect of benefit is *effectiveness*[1], or yield: the percentage of the defects present in a work product that your inspections discover (Gilb and Graham 1993; Humphrey 1995). Another aspect is *efficiency:* the effort required to find a defect by inspection. A third measure of impact is the *return on investment* your organization is obtaining from its inspection program.

Effectiveness

Inspection effectiveness is a lagging indicator: you can't measure it at the time of the inspection, only at a later time. Calculating effectiveness requires that you count both the defects your inspections discover and those found in later development or testing stages and by customers. Defects found by customers within three to six months following product release provide a reasonable indication of how many significant defects eluded your quality nets. To illustrate an inspection

---

[1]Some authors, such as Capers Jones (2000), use the term "efficiency" for this measure.

effectiveness calculation, consider the following sample data for a single code module:

Defects found during code inspection:	7
Defects found during unit testing:	3
Defects found during system testing:	2
Defects found by customer:	1
Total defects initially present in the code:	13

Code inspection effectiveness: 100 * (7 defects found by inspection) /
   (13 defects total) = 54%

If you know your inspection effectiveness, you can estimate how many defects remain in a document following inspection. Suppose that your average effectiveness for inspecting requirements specifications is 60 percent and that you found 16 major defects while inspecting a particular specification. Assuming that the average applies to this inspection, you can estimate that the document originally contained about 27 major defects, of which 11 remain to be discovered by some other means later on. Without knowing your inspection effectiveness, you can't make any claims about the quality of a document following inspection.

Combining your inspection effectiveness and the document size with the number of defects found by inspecting a small sample of a document lets you estimate the total number of defects in the rest of the document. This is a bit oversimplified because it assumes that the sample is representative of the whole document and that the inspection is 100 percent effective, which is probably not the case. To estimate the potential cost of those remaining defects, multiply the defect count estimate by your average cost of correcting defects found through system testing or by customers. (If you don't know these average costs, begin collecting them now.) Compare that projected cost with the cost of inspecting the rest of the document to judge whether such inspection is warranted economically.

Using some typical numbers, the following example suggests that it would be cheaper to remove the remaining defects by inspection (90 labor hours) than by system testing (270 labor hours). This illustration assumes that testing and inspection find the same types of bugs, but that also might not be the case.

Defects found in a 2-page sample of 20 pages of source code:	2 defects
Estimated defects in the remaining 18 pages:	18 defects
Effort spent inspecting the 2-page sample:	10 labor hours

Estimated effort to inspect the remaining 18 pages:	$5 * 18 = 90$ labor hours
Average effort to find and correct a defect in system test:	15 labor hours
Estimated effort needed to find and correct the remaining 18 defects by system testing:	$15 * 18 = 270$ labor hours

Effective inspections lead to fewer defects being found during later-stage testing. Introducing code inspections at Nortel Networks reduced the number of defects found per test case during functional verification by more than 80 percent (Naccache and Ghaemi 1999). However, if your testing starts to reveal fewer bugs, someone might inappropriately conclude that testing is less effective than it used to be for some reason. Interpret your data carefully to understand trends and underlying causes before taking any potentially counterproductive action for misguided reasons.

Efficiency

The more efficient your inspections are, the more defects they discover per hour of effort. When you begin holding inspections, strive to maximize efficiency, which reduces the average cost of finding a defect. There's a paradox here, though. A successful inspection program leads to process improvements that reduce the number of errors developers make, thereby leaving fewer defects in the deliverables to be discovered by inspection or testing. So, as your product quality improves, the cost of discovering each defect will *increase,* and the trends in your metrics will become harder to interpret (Bianco 1996). Monitor both inspection efficiency and effectiveness to understand whether a trend toward decreasing efficiency truly indicates higher product quality, or if it means your inspections are not working as well as they should be. You might reach a point where the increased cost of using inspections to hunt for the few defects present in the product exceeds the business risks of shipping the product with those defects still present.

Return on Investment

The return on investment from inspections provides a quantitative cost/benefit analysis. Inspection authority Don O'Neill defines inspection ROI as follows (O'Neill 1996):

$$\text{Return on Investment} \quad = \quad \frac{\text{Net savings}}{\text{Detection cost}}$$

The net savings from a specific defect is the estimated cost of fixing it at some point in the future minus the actual cost of fixing it whenever you did detect it. The detection cost is the actual cost of your inspection. Net savings and detection cost could both be measured either in labor hours or in actual dollars.

If your ROI is less than 1, it is difficult to justify inspections. Remember, though, that inspections provide a multitude of benefits in addition to cost savings through early defect detection. The rewards from cross-training, defect prevention through process improvements, and increased customer good will are real but difficult to quantify.

The net savings to the development team from an inspection are the costs that your team avoided by finding defects early, rather than late. Because you *did* find the defects through inspection, you don't know exactly what it would have cost you to find those same defects later. However, if you know the average cost of finding and fixing a defect during system testing or in operation, you can estimate the potential savings from each defect that you find by inspection. There is an additional benefit for the customer, who won't be affected by a bug you removed through inspection. Again, this is difficult to quantify.

Suppose you think that a major defect discovered during a requirements specification inspection would otherwise have been reported by the customer. Here's how you could compute your ROI for that one defect, using some sample figures:

Average effort to process and correct a major customer-reported requirement defect:	40 labor hours
Average effort to repair and verify a major requirement defect found by inspection:	0.5 labor hour
Net savings:	39.5 labor hours
Average effort per major requirement defect found by inspection:	2 labor hours
Return on investment:	39.5 / 2 = 19.75

In practice, you would perform such calculations for a set of defects, not on an individual basis. Robert Grady of Hewlett-Packard Company (1992, 1997) provided a detailed description of how to estimate the savings from inspections by considering coding productivity, initial defect density, cost to find and fix defects at different life-cycle stages, inspection rates, and other factors.

The simple calculation just shown considers only the effort involved in a single inspection. It ignores the other real costs of your peer review program, including training the team, defining and maintaining the review process and its process assets, developing and maintaining the infrastructure, and analyzing review data. Some of these are one-time startup costs, while others are ongoing investments of time expended by the peer review process owner and the review coordinator. A complete ROI analysis over a specified period of time must include these initial and ongoing expenses along with the cost of the inspections themselves. The ROI will increase over time, both because your team will become better at inspection and because you will amortize your initial investment in training and process infrastructure development.

Suppose a manager asks for the expected ROI when you're getting started, before you've had time to collect your own data. You'll have to rely on literature data, without knowing how accurately the published experiences from other companies model your own prospective results. A general heuristic is that each major defect that is not found by inspection requires an average of about nine to ten hours to correct later on (Gilb and Graham 1993; Grady 1997). If an average of one labor hour of effort is needed to find each major defect, the net savings amounts to about eight or nine hours per defect found, less the effort to correct each major defect found by inspection. This potential benefit should impress even the most determined skeptic.

How many defects will your inspectors find? No one knows. Badly conducted inspections won't pay for themselves and they'll leave a negative impression in the minds of the participants and their managers. However, many organizations have saved considerable effort through software inspections. The National Software Quality Experiment has collected practitioner data on software quality since 1992. Most of the 78 organizations that have participated to date achieved a return on investment from inspections of between 2:1 and 8:1, so impressive results are clearly possible (O'Neill 2001). One information technology organization that trained nearly 500 practitioners in inspection achieved an ROI of about 7:1 for code inspections and as high as 14:1 for inspections of requirements and design documents (Mah 2001).

These substantial savings provide an excellent counterargument to resisters who fear that inspections will slow the project down. Even if you don't achieve such dramatic results initially, the ROI only has to be a little greater than 1.0 to make inspections worth doing.

CHAPTER TEN

Installing a
Peer Review Program

S imply knowing the mechanics of inspections and other types of peer reviews doesn't guarantee that everyone will perform them routinely or effectively. A successful review program needs a solid cultural foundation and process infrastructure. This chapter describes how to implement a review program through training, staffing, and development of essential process assets. These assets include a process description, peer review policy, forms, and other work aids. Process improvement is always a challenge. When it succeeds, though, the long-term benefits far outweigh the short-term sacrifice.

The Peer Review Process Owner

Every software organization should identify a *process owner* for each of its key processes, including its peer review program (Paulk et al. 1995; Zahran 1998). Process owners usually should be managers, although a senior process engineer can fill this role in an organization that has an established software process improvement program. Look for a manager who strongly believes in reviews and is willing to devote energy to making the program succeed. The process owner provides continuity, serving as the point of contact for requests to improve the review procedures, forms, and checklists. Without ownership, processes can decay over time and fail to meet the organization's current needs.

Software process improvement typically involves a small working group of part-time stakeholders who develop new or improved processes in a specific technical area. The working group is often chartered, and perhaps partially staffed, by members of the organization's *software engineering process group,* which coordinates process improvement activities. The working group pilots the new process, makes adjustments based on the pilot results, and rolls the process out to the organization. The working group then disbands, its task complete. Too often, the process improvement actions stop there; busy practitioners aren't going to change how they work just because some of their colleagues recommend a different approach. Additionally, if no one has responsibility for adjusting the process, improvements won't be made when the early adopters encounter problems.

The process owner role addresses these concerns. The peer review process owner is an enthusiastic, committed champion, a sustaining sponsor who serves as the organization's authority for the peer review program (Gilb and Graham 1993). As senior management's delegate, he sets expectations for how and when reviews will be conducted through a peer review policy. Figure 10–1 lists typical responsibilities of the peer review process owner (Litton 2000).

Preparing the Organization

Change can be frightening, exciting, intimidating, motivating, and upsetting— sometimes all at once. When you ask people to work in new ways, they'll want to know why they need to change, what problems the changes will solve, what you expect of them, and what's in it for them. Be prepared to answer those questions regarding your proposed review program.

First, explain why you want to implement peer reviews. "Because it's a good thing to do" will satisfy those engineers who understand sound software engineering principles. "Because we have the following problems and we think reviews will help us in the following ways" is a more convincing argument. Expect to hear, "We're already too busy; we don't have time for reviews," both as a genuine concern and as a sign of resistance. Explain to the protesters that if we shift some of the effort we currently spend on rework (which is largely invisible) to performing reviews that prevent rework, we'll come out ahead. Chapter 2 described common reasons for resistance to reviews and suggested ways to address them.

Assure your team members that you intend to implement the review program in a way that maximizes the benefits and minimizes the impact on tight project schedules. Communication reduces the barriers to change, as does engaging team

---

Peer Review Process Owner Responsibilities

❑ Maintain expert knowledge of peer reviews and the details of the local review process.

❑ Establish and enforce review policies.

❑ Charter the peer review program and define its vision, scope, and strategy.

❑ Convene the peer review working group and coordinate its activities.

❑ Lead the writing of an action plan to define and install the review process.

❑ Arrange for training in reviews as needed.

❑ Determine how to reward the early adopters of the review program and reinforce the desired review participant behaviors. Convey reward recommendations to other managers.

❑ Monitor the practice of peer reviews on projects and evaluate their effectiveness.

❑ Propagate successful implementations of the review program throughout the organization.

❑ Define the necessary peer review data items and metrics and set expectations for collecting and using these metrics.

❑ Use review metrics data to identify improvements to make in the review process and in other engineering and quality processes.

❑ Review process modification requests and implement approved requests.

❑ Ensure that the organization's process assets library contains the baselined peer review process description, process assets, and training materials.

❑ Maintain a list of tools that support the peer review process.

Figure 10–1. Peer review process owner responsibilities

members in developing and trying out the new process. Some members of the team will be enthusiastic supporters, eager to participate and happy to help. Enlist these early adopters as allies. The majority will be skeptical and cautious, concerned about the time demands, about doing something different, and about the threat of misuse of the reviews for punishment. Training, communication, and early success stories help to allay those fears. A few diehards will choose to lie across the railroad tracks of progress in an attempt to block your review efforts. Don't waste a lot of energy trying to convert people who aren't going to be willing review participants no matter what you say or do. The train is coming through; they can get on board or get out of the way.

Pain is a powerful motivator for change. You should be able to describe the pain your development team, company, and customers experience because of quality or productivity shortcomings and explain how peer reviews can help. A process improvement effort launched as an outgrowth of analyzing a recent painful failure provides a powerful stimulus for performing reviews. You don't need detailed metrics to describe such pain. For example, one company observed that its products did not meet its target market's quality expectations. This was a serious concern, because word-of-mouth recommendations were a significant factor in the company's ability to increase sales, and unhappy customers don't say nice things about the product. Management concluded that they could not realistically rectify their quality shortcomings on the back end of development by adding more testers. Instead, they chose to inspect selected design and code components to help engineers catch problems in their complex products prior to testing.

Your team won't reap the full potential benefits when they begin performing peer reviews. Inspection authority Don O'Neill (1997) suggests that properly trained inspectors can immediately begin finding about half of the defects present in their work products. As the inspectors gain experience over the next 12 to 18 months, their defect detection efficiency should increase to between 60 and 90 percent.

Figure 10–2 depicts the inescapable learning curve—sometimes called the J-curve of technology adoption—that everyone must climb when implementing new practices (Wiegers 1999). The learning curve results in an initial performance drop (performance is usually measured as productivity) as the team develops its review process assets and infrastructure, attends training sessions, conducts a pilot, and begins holding reviews. These activities consume energy that some people think could be better spent on coding. It is tempting to abandon the fledgling review program at the lowest point in the curve, after you've made the investment but before you've given the new techniques a chance to pay off. If you can keep the faith long enough for practitioners to begin getting tangible results from their reviews, you can push through the learning curve and improve your team's performance. It takes time, though. Don't expect the first project that uses reviews to get fabulously improved results, especially if they review only code and not the earlier life-cycle deliverables.

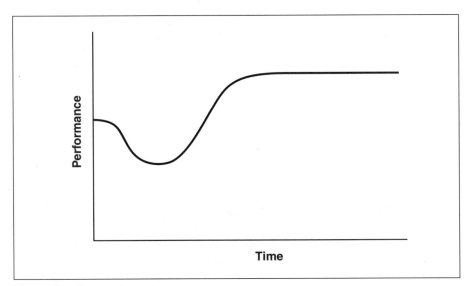

Figure 10–2. The learning curve

Several additional factors contribute to establishing and sustaining a new process in a software organization. First, you need a ***documented process***. The next section of this chapter recommends components of your peer review process description and identifies other process assets you'll need for the program to succeed.

If you're serious about incorporating reviews into routine use, issue a ***written review policy***. Dedicated practitioners don't need an organizational policy to motivate them to apply effective software engineering practices. However, a review policy issued by senior management through the process owner sets a clear direction for performing reviews in an organization (Gilb and Graham 1993; Paulk et al. 1995). This policy indicates that reviewers will be trained and states management expectations about which projects will conduct reviews, when the reviews will be performed, and which work products will be reviewed. Each project team is expected to keep records about the reviews they perform, and the policy should state that management will not use this data to evaluate individuals. If you issue such a review policy, make sure it is broadly communicated and enforced. A policy without accountability is merely a suggestion.

A meaningful policy demands ***management commitment*** at all levels. If your project manager isn't interested in reviews despite the organizational policy, you'll conduct reviews only if they are personally important to you. Reviews also demand visible *practitioner support* across the organization. Your team members are either serious about improving quality through peer reviews or they are not. People who are reluctant to participate in reviews or to have their own work reviewed undermine the efforts of others.

Your review effort won't succeed unless the team has adequate *resources and training*. Resources include tools, databases, and funds for training. Most critical is allocated staff time, including effort devoted by the process owner, review coordinator, working group, and, of course, the reviewers themselves. There's no perfect, painless time to introduce process changes. Commencing reviews on a project that is already underway can be a bit disruptive, but you have to start somewhere.

As Chapter 9 indicated, *measurement* of selected aspects of your review activities provides valuable insights. These measurements include collecting a variety of data to understand how well your reviews are working. Don't let measurement—or the fear of measurement—become an obstacle to getting your review program started, though. Holding reviews without data collection is more valuable than not holding reviews at all.

The bottom line from any process improvement effort is that the team members apply the new practices routinely, not just when it is convenient or when someone reminds them. They hold reviews because they know the reviews are powerful contributors to project success. *Verification* that reviews are being performed as intended and yielding the desired results confirms the success of your peer review program. Verification involves tracking reviews actually held against those that were planned, checking to see that the reviewers are following the defined process, and judging how effective that process is.

Implementing process change isn't cheap. The initial costs of your review program include the time and money you spend to:

- Define the review process
- Create forms, defect checklists, rule sets, and other work aids
- Train the participants
- Pilot the review process
- Set up a repository to store review data and permit data analysis and reporting

These start-up costs feed into the initial downward slope of the learning curve, when you're making an investment that you expect to be more than repaid out of the cost savings from early defect detection. The program's ongoing costs include the time that the process owner and review coordinator spend to monitor the review activities, work with the data, and refine the process over time. The greatest cost is the time that team members spend actually performing peer reviews. View this not as an added project burden but as part of what it takes to build high-quality software efficiently.

Process Assets

Don't expect your team members to perform peer reviews effectively unless they have a written process description and supporting work aids, collectively termed *process assets*. The process must be clear and easy to apply, or people won't use it. Someone at a conference once told me that his organization was having a hard time getting its inspection program going. When I learned that their inspection procedure was more than fifty pages long, I wasn't surprised they were having problems. While this wasn't the only contributing factor, concise and pragmatic process documentation reduces the resistance level.

It is often convenient to deliver your process documentation through an intranet site, breaking it into logical portions so users can access just the components they need. Include hyperlinks to the pertinent checklists, forms, and other work aids. A problem with using HTML to deliver the process components is that assembling a complete and nicely formatted process description is difficult. I have found it valuable to also provide the complete process description as a single document in PDF format, but this does increase the process documentation maintenance effort.

Figure 10–3 identifies some items to include in your peer review process. The process overview provides a high-level description of the activities involved in any type of review. One of those steps is to select an appropriate review method for each situation. A well-documented process includes procedures with step-by-step instructions for performing several types of peer reviews. An inspection procedure will be the longest and most detailed. You might also create written procedures or checklists for informal reviews such as peer deskchecks if you are concerned about inconsistency in the way people perform them.

You can access a sample peer review process description from the Web site that accompanies this book; see Appendix B. The sample process includes procedures for performing inspections, walkthroughs, and passarounds. Each procedure description includes the following elements: participants and their roles, entry criteria, tasks and responsible participants, deliverables, verification activities (if any), and

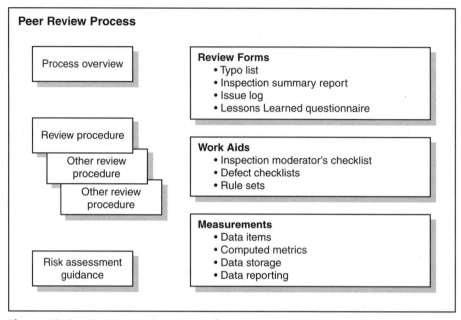

Figure 10–3. Contents of a peer review process

exit criteria. Write procedures as though your readers are experts in the technique being described. This keeps the procedures short and makes them a handy quick reference for someone who just wants to see the steps to follow. If needed, provide additional tutorial or philosophical information in separate reference documents.

The process description should tell the reader where to access electronic copies of the following review forms and work aids, preferably through hyperlinks embedded in the process description:

- Typo list (Chapter 6)
- Inspection summary report (Chapter 7)
- Issue log (Chapter 7)
- Lessons Learned questionnaire (Chapter 7)
- Inspection moderator's checklist (Chapter 7)
- Defect checklists, rule sets, and other analysis tools (Chapter 6)

The process also describes the data items to be collected, the metrics you will compute from these data items, and the mechanisms for storing and reporting on the data. Your data collection, storage, and analysis will become more sophisticated as you gain experience. You might switch from a simple spreadsheet with a few charting macros to a full-featured database having advanced analysis and reporting capabilities.

The first generation of your peer review process need not include all the elements shown in Figure 10–3. You might begin with an inspection procedure and add a walkthrough procedure later on. Perhaps you'll elect not to collect review measurements at the outset. At a minimum, start with one review procedure and the basic review forms. Feedback from process users might lead you to change the recommended participants for inspections of specific deliverable types, modify the forms, or adjust the procedures. Rather than trying to devise the ultimate review process right out of the gate, start with a nonintimidating process that provides a solid foundation on which your review program can grow.

The Peer Review Coordinator

In addition to the process owner—the management sponsor who champions the peer review program—organizations should identify an individual to coordinate the program on a day-to-day basis. Typically this is a part-time responsibility performed by a software quality engineer or perhaps by the validation coordinator in an organization that creates products for regulated industries. Large organizations might assign a peer review coordinator to each major project. Because this role will consume considerable time, it should be clearly defined as part of the coordinator's primary job description. The same person could fill both the peer review coordinator and process owner roles. However, the process owner should ordinarily be a manager who probably won't have the time for ongoing program coordination.

The ideal peer review coordinator is an experienced inspector and moderator who thoroughly understands the technical and social aspects of reviews. He coaches team members who need help performing reviews and works with the process owner to maximize the program's effectiveness. The coordinator schedules—and possibly conducts—training sessions for new reviewers as needed. He is the custodian of the organization's inspection database. Moderators give him the size, time, effort, and defect data from their inspections, and he generates summary reports and analyzes the metrics. Based on this data analysis, the coordinator offers process improvement suggestions.

Although the peer review coordinator can moderate the initial inspections, project teams eventually must adopt responsibility for conducting their own inspections, using their own moderators. Think of the review coordinator as supplying training wheels to get the peer review program rolling and providing expert guidance. If you have a pool of qualified moderators, the coordinator can assign one to each inspection that an author requests. The coordinator should observe reviews periodically to see how the process works in practice. He works with moderators to diagnose and rectify inspection problems. For example, if participants repeatedly come unprepared to inspection meetings, he needs to know why before he can take suitable corrective actions. Are inspectors receiving the materials early enough to permit adequate preparation? Do they understand how important preparation is and know how to prepare? Can they choose and apply appropriate analysis techniques? Once the coordinator understands the underlying cause, he can determine how best to address the problem.

Peer Review Training

Although the information in this book is enough to get you started, potential review participants (and people who don't read the book) will benefit from training in the concepts and practices of peer reviews. The training should include at least one practice inspection. You also need to educate your team about your organization's specific peer review processes and policies. New people who join the group might also need training, so try to make the class available on an as-needed basis. After completing their training, all participants should be able to:

- Explain why peer reviews add value at all stages of software development
- Describe the differences between formal and informal reviews
- List the participants in an inspection and describe their roles
- Describe the activities performed at each inspection stage
- Summarize the guidelines for conducting a successful review
- List several important inspection metrics
- Participate effectively in inspections and less formal peer reviews

Training can both educate and motivate. After one student attended a class I taught, she asked some of her colleagues to inspect part of the code for a completed project. Although the team had already concluded that the product was acceptable, the inspection revealed two new major defects. This group now strongly believes in the value of performing inspections *before* they think development is complete. Another former student said that he and some colleagues persuaded a talented but arrogant teammate ("*my* work doesn't need reviewing") to submit some code for review. While the reviewers detected no major errors, they found enough minor problems that their teammate now willingly participates in reviews and appreciates their value.

Table 10–1 presents an outline for a one-day seminar on peer reviews targeted at potential review participants. Organizations with an established peer review program can perhaps get by with a shorter training session. During the practice inspection, the class breaks into teams of four to seven people each. Volunteers take the key inspection roles of moderator, reader, author (simulated), and recorder, with any additional participants serving simply as extra inspectors. Several participants receive special role-playing instructions to try to lead the team down an unconstructive path and give the moderator a chance to bring the meeting back on course. Students find the practice inspection session realistic, enlightening, and enjoyable.

Table 10–1. Suggested Outline for One-Day Training Seminar on Peer Reviews

Minutes	*Topic*
60	Introduction to Peer Reviews
	• Definition of reviews
	• Objectives of peer reviews
	• Why people don't do reviews
	• Cultural barriers to peer reviews
	• Building reviews into the project plan
	• What can be reviewed
	• Using risk to select items to review
	• Relative cost of fixing defects
	• Some actual benefits from inspections
	• Reviews and capability maturity models
	• Detecting defects through testing or reviews
120	Software Inspections
	• Informal and formal reviews
	• Peer review formality spectrum
	• Who should inspect what
	• Software inspections
	• Entry criteria
	• Inspection participant roles
	• Desirable moderator characteristics
	• Managers and observers
	• The inspection process

(*continued*)

Table 10–1. **Suggested Outline for One-Day Training Seminar on Peer Reviews (*cont.*)**

Minutes	Topic
	• Inspection rates • The inspection package • Defect checklists, rules, and analysis methods • Inspection stage descriptions • Exit criteria • Inspection summary report • Issue log • Typo list • Inspection metrics
15	Overview Meeting for Practice Inspection
30	Preparation for Practice Inspection
45	Other Peer Review Methods • Descriptions of other peer review methods • Pluses and minuses of formal reviews • Pluses and minuses of informal reviews • Selecting an appropriate review method
60	Making Reviews Work for You • Guidelines for effective peer reviews • Videotape: "Scenes of Software Inspections" • Critical success factors for reviews • Documenting your peer review process • The process owner and peer review coordinator • Inspection best practices • Review traps to avoid
75	Practice Inspection Meeting and Debriefing

The practice inspection could use one of the project team's actual work products, provided that no one would be uncomfortable or embarrassed. Otherwise, a sample requirements specification or a program written in a language that all of the seminar attendees know will suffice. Sometimes I inject several artificial, yet plausible errors into the real work product being inspected. Knowing that defects have been seeded makes the students more willing to point out things they think might be wrong. The reaction is interesting when a student points out a defect and asks hopefully whether it was one I inserted, only to be told that it was an actual error in their own deliverable. This experience reinforces two important points: their work products do indeed contain defects, and they can find many of them by inspection.

A useful training aid is a videotape called "Scenes of Software Inspections: Video Dramatizations for the Classroom," which is available from the Software Engineering Institute (Deimel 1991). The videotape presents several short scenes of actors portraying typical inspection experiences. The scenes are informative and students find them entertaining as well. An accompanying technical report includes a discussion guide to help the instructor use this videotape in a training setting.

People who will serve as moderators should receive one to two days of additional training, depending on their previous experience with inspections and similar activities. The additional time emphasizes the moderator's inspection responsibilities and covers such important moderator skills as meeting management, decision-making, facilitation, listening skills, and conflict management. The training should permit all students to practice moderating an inspection. Many organizations allow only individuals who have gone through such specialized instruction to be certified as moderators. Additional post-training certification steps might require the candidate moderator to observe an actual inspection and then to moderate one while an experienced moderator observes. The observer either certifies the candidate as a qualified moderator or recommends additional coaching, training, or practice. Consider having your review coordinator serve as the moderator certifier, monitoring each new moderator's performance for a while until he is fully proficient.

After teaching hundreds of software seminars, I have seen most frequently on evaluation forms the comments "My manager needs to take this class," "I can't do this unless my manager buys in," and "Where's my manager?" It's demoralizing for developers to walk out of a seminar motivated to use new software practices, only to face resistance from a manager who doesn't understand or value the new techniques. Managers should attend a half-day presentation on peer reviews, although it's even better if they can participate in the same training seminar their team members take.

Training doesn't guarantee a successful review program. The review coordinator and process owner need to follow up after the training to make sure the team is actually performing reviews and achieving useful results. The best indicators that your process is working are that the reviews actually find bugs and that authors improve their deliverables with input from their colleagues. A survey of review participants after several months will reveal how team members feel about the review program and point out problems to address. Understanding the review procedures and guidelines lays the foundation, and experience improves the results, especially if someone is available to coach and provide feedback on the early reviews.

Piloting the Review Process

New processes that look good on paper often require adjustment in practice. The first process a working group defines might be too complicated, be inadequately supported with suitable work aids, or fail to work as intended. Pilot your review process with some willing early adopters before rolling it out to the entire organization (Gilb and Graham 1993). A pilot is an experiment, testing the hypothesis that the new process is adequately defined, practical, and suitable for your organization. A new process and its accompanying process assets will evolve further as the team gains experience following the pilot, but the pilot leads to a workable process that gets the team started.

I once participated in a review of an organization's new peer review process. The authors rejected my suggestion that we use the peer review process to review the peer review process (software people can handle such recursion). While this wouldn't have sufficed as a complete pilot experience, the group missed an excellent opportunity to test their new, theoretically perfect process. Even if you don't perform a formal pilot, start with just one project and share its results with the rest of the organization.

A pilot involves several peer reviews in which the participants carefully follow the new process to see how well it works in operation. Pilots should examine substantive work products, rather than wasting time practicing on inconsequential documents. Select pilot reviews that examine different types of work products so you can try out several checklists, analysis methods, and reading techniques. Use the pilots to resolve any open issues that the review's working group might have had. The review coordinator can use data collected from pilot reviews to try out the data entry, analysis, and reporting tools. The results from a small-scale pilot can help you convince managers and practitioners of the benefits of peer reviews and obtain the commitment needed for a sustainable review program.

The process owner should discuss the pilot experiences with the participants and see that the process is modified if necessary. After tuning things up, you're ready to roll the peer review process out to your project teams and begin to enjoy the many benefits of peer reviews—but respect the learning curve.

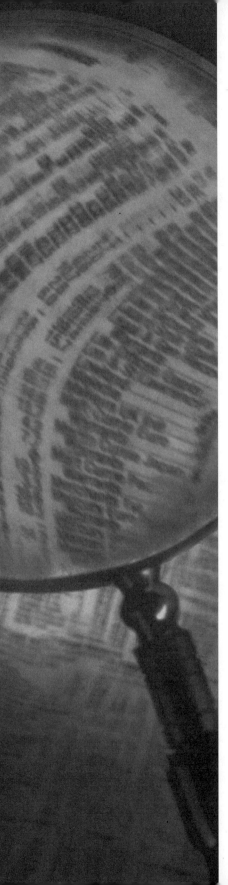

CHAPTER ELEVEN

Making Peer Reviews Work for You

Weaving peer reviews into the cultural fabric of an organization takes time. A new review process is fragile, being easily disrupted by unpleasant experiences ("my reviewers treated me like an idiot") or ineffective results ("we wasted all that time and didn't find a single major defect"). This chapter describes several factors that make a review program work (see Figure 11–1) and points out several review traps to avoid. A troubleshooting guide at the end of the chapter helps you diagnose and rectify review problems.

Critical Success Factors

The people involved and their attitude toward quality are the greatest contributors to a review program's success. The first critical factor is for your team members to prefer to *have peers, rather than customers, find defects* (Wiegers 1996a). Your "customers" include anyone whose work is based on your deliverable, such as a test engineer who will design tests from a requirements specification. Practitioners must appreciate the many benefits that peer reviews can provide, including early defect removal, reduced late-stage rework, document quality assessment, cross-training, and process improvements for defect prevention (Gilb 2000). Once your team members understand cost-of-quality and return-on-investment concepts, they can overcome barriers such as the perception that adding reviews to the project schedule delays delivery.

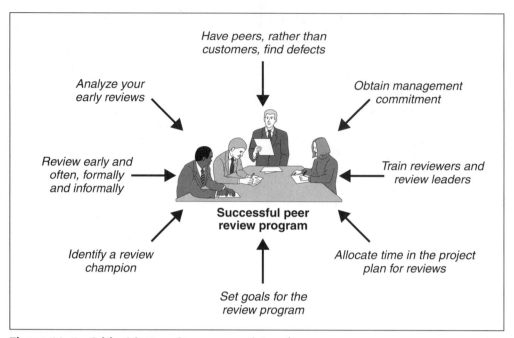

Figure 11–1. Critical factors for a successful review program

Even motivated team members will struggle to perform reviews if you don't *obtain management commitment*. Commitment isn't simply a matter of giving permission or saying "Everybody do reviews." As Chapter 2 pointed out, management commitment includes establishing policies and goals; providing resources, time, training, and recognition; and abiding by the review team's decisions.

A third critical element is to *train reviewers and review leaders,* as well as the managers of projects that are conducting reviews. Forty-eight percent of the respondents to a survey indicated that untrained practitioners impeded their initial use of inspections (Brykczynski 1994). Training can teach people why and how to perform inspections, but only experience enables them to provide and receive insightful comments.

Be sure to *allocate time in the project plan for reviews* and rework. Despite their good intentions, swamped practitioners will skimp on reviews when time pressures mount. This leads to even greater time pressure in upcoming months as the latent defects become evident. Devoting several percent of a project's effort to peer reviews is a powerful sign of management's commitment to quality.

Groups in which I have worked found it valuable to *set goals for the review program*. One team committed to reviewing 100 percent of its requirements specifications, 60 percent of design documents, 75 percent of the code, and so on (Wiegers 1996a). Setting numerical goals forced us to track the quantity of each kind of artifact we created so we could measure progress toward our goals. We achieved our goals, and in the process ingrained peer review as a routine practice. A more advanced goal involves defining quantitative targets for the estimated number of defects remaining in work products that exit an inspection. This will stimulate detailed inspection and quality measurement. Another goal might be to reduce your rework levels from a known starting point to a specified lower percentage of your total development effort. Make sure your review goals are attainable, measurable, and aligned with your organization's objectives.

Next, *identify a review champion,* perhaps yourself, who has personally experienced the benefits. The champion serves as a local advocate, speaking from experience rather than from theoretical knowledge. A review champion who is respected by other team members—whether he is a technical peer, a manager, or a quality engineer—can break down the initial resistance to peer reviews. A highly capable developer who invites reviews sends the signal that everyone can benefit from input from his colleagues.

Plan to *review early and often, formally and informally*. Use the cheapest review method that will satisfy your objectives for each situation and each work product. A quick ad hoc review sometimes suffices. At other times, you will need the diverse perspectives that a passaround provides, the brainstorming of a walk-through, the structure of a team review, or the rigor of an inspection. Informal, incremental reviews of a work product under development can filter out many defects quickly and cheaply. One risk is that the reviewers might tire of examining the same document repeatedly, perhaps starting to feel that they're doing the author's work. Another risk of reviewing early is that you'll have to repeat the review because of modifications made after other documents have changed. Nonetheless, using multiple types of reviews in sequence provides a powerful way to improve document quality.

Your first reviews won't go as well as you'd like (remember the learning curve from Figure 10–2). To improve their effectiveness, *analyze your early reviews*. Use the inspection Lessons Learned questionnaire from Figure 7–5 to see where the process needs tuning. Continuously improve your peer review procedures, checklists, and forms based on experience. Incorporate the best known inspection practices, such as those in Figure 11–2, into your process.

Some Software Inspection Best Practices

- Plan inspections to address your project and inspection objectives.
- Use serious, quantitative entry and exit conditions.
- Inspect upstream documents first.
- Begin inspecting documents early in their lives.
- Check against source and related documents.
- Prepare and inspect at your organization's optimum rates.
- Focus on major defects.
- Measure your benefits from inspections.
- Emphasize defect prevention and process improvement.

Figure 11–2. Some software inspection best practices (Gilb 1998, 2000).

Review Traps to Avoid

Several traps can undermine the success of a peer review program (Lee 1997; Wiegers 1998). These problems occur most commonly with inspections; informal reviews that lack a defined process aren't susceptible to having the process be misunderstood or not followed. Many of these problems arise when an inspection moderator is not doing an effective job.

Trap #1: Participants don't understand the review process. One symptom of this trap is that team members do not use an accurate, consistent vocabulary to describe peer reviews of various types. Another clue is that review teams do not follow a consistent process. Training and a practical, documented peer review process are essential. All potential reviewers must understand the what, why, when, how, and who of reviews. Stephen Allott's description of the habits of highly effective inspection teams provides an insightful experience report (Allott 1999). These habits include the following:

- Put the inspection above your own work.
- Choose inspectors carefully.
- Effort, endeavor, and excellence are required from the inspectors.
- Control the discussion to log defects at the optimum rate.
- Trust the author, but check the fixes.
- Keep the metrics confidential.

Trap #2: The review process isn't followed. Before taking corrective action, learn why the process isn't being followed. After you have diagnosed the underlying causes, select appropriate actions to get the review program into gear. If the process is too complex, practitioners might abandon it or perform reviews in some other way instead. If your managers have not conveyed their expectations through a policy, practitioners will perform reviews only when it's convenient or personally important to them. If quality is not a success driver for a project, the quality benefits of peer reviews won't provide a compelling argument for performing them. However, the productivity enhancements that reviews can provide might support a project goal of meeting an aggressive delivery schedule. Introducing reviews on a project that is already in deep trouble with schedule overruns, churning requirements, and tired developers will be hard, but it will be worth the effort if the reviews help get the project back on track.

Trap #3: The right people do not participate. Inappropriate participants include managers who came without being invited by the author and observers who attend without a clear objective. While you can include a few participants who are there primarily to learn, focus on inviting reviewers who will find problems.

Table 5–1 recommended some project roles that should participate in inspections of various types of deliverables. One person will perform several roles on a small project, so invite some colleagues to represent the other points of view. Some reviews will be crippled if key perspectives are not represented. As an example, a requirements specification review needs the customer's viewpoint to judge correctness and completeness and to resolve ambiguities and conflicts quickly. The customer could be represented by actual end users or by surrogates such as marketing staff. To underscore the need for the right participants, below is an e-mail I received from one of my consulting clients, describing her experiences with requirements specification reviews:

> *The reviews were extremely helpful, especially given that the users were in-house and were very motivated to influence project decisions. User contributions to the requirements reviews were highly valued by all participants. We canceled more than one review for lack of user participation, and I remember one review where we called in a user unexpectedly because the others had failed to show up. The one who came had no preparation time, and we delayed the start of the meeting waiting for her to show up, but she provided very valuable insights and suggestions nevertheless. User participation in the reviews*

was an unqualified success and led to software that was more valued by its users and to a better working relationship between the project and the users.

Trap #4: Review meetings drift into problem-solving. Unless a review has been specifically invoked as a brainstorming session, the group should focus on finding—not fixing—errors. When a review meeting switches to finding solutions, the process of examining the product comes to a halt. Participants tune out if they aren't fascinated by the problem being discussed. When the reviewers realize the meeting time is almost up, they hastily flip through the remaining pages and declare the review a success. In reality, the material they glossed over likely contains major problems that will haunt the development team in the future. Moderator failure is the prime contributor to this problem.

Trap #5: Reviewers focus on style, not substance. An issue log that lists only style problems suggests that the reviewers were distracted by style, were not adequately prepared, or did only a superficial examination. To avoid this trap, define coding standards and adopt standard templates for other project documents. Coding standards address layout, naming conventions, commenting, language constructs to avoid, and other factors that enhance readability and maintainability. As part of judging whether a work product satisfies its inspection entry criteria, have a standards checker see if it conforms to the pertinent standard. Use code reformatting tools (a feature found in some source code editors) to enforce layout standards automatically. Standardizing code layouts will help reviewers focus on the important logical, functional, and semantic issues.

Troubleshooting Review Problems

With planning and perseverance, you should be able to install an effective software peer review program in your organization. Sometimes, though, difficulties arise. Table 11–1 lists several review problems you might encounter, along with suggestions for dealing with each. These possible solutions will be of most help to the peer review coordinator and other local review champions. There's no guarantee that a specific solution will do the trick, particularly if the underlying problems are cultural, political, or emotional in nature. People who strongly oppose the review program can damage it, but don't be held captive by the most recalcitrant members of your organization. If managers and opinion leaders instill pride of craftsmanship and an appreciation of software engineering best practices in the organization, most team members will give reviews a try. They'll be glad they did.

Table 11–1. Symptoms and Solutions for Common Review Problems

Symptoms	*Possible Solutions*
Cultural Issues	
Some team members refuse to have their work reviewed.	• Understand the factors underlying the resistance so you can deal with them. The actions you take will depend on what you learn. • Provide all team members with peer review training. Explain that all professionals can benefit from having their work reviewed through defect discovery, process improvement, and sharing of their knowledge and experience with others. • Start with informal reviews such as peer deskchecks or passarounds. • Make sure your review process suits the culture. Modify it if portions are unpalatable to team members. Any review is better than none. • Have management reward review participants and authors to reinforce the desired behaviors. • Conduct reviews in a constructive, safe, and professional fashion to reduce the threat they pose to an author's self-image. • Obtain a promise from management not to misuse data collected from reviews to evaluate individuals. Ensure that review data is protected from inappropriate access. • Establish an organizational policy that lists the work products to be reviewed and expects all authors of those products to make their work available for review as scheduled. • Steer the culture toward routine performance of peer reviews as a job expectation. Hold team members accountable for participating in reviews as part of their professional responsibilities to the project team.

(continued)

Table 11–1. Symptoms and Solutions for Common Review Problems (*cont.*)

Symptoms	*Possible Solutions*
Some team members refuse to review other people's work.	• Provide all team members with training in peer reviews. • Explain that software development is a team effort. The effort they spend to help improve a colleague's deliverables provides benefits to developers creating deliverables later in the life-cycle and to product support staff, the company, and your customers. • Build review participation into team member job descriptions. • Hold all team members accountable for participating in reviews as part of their professional responsibilities to the project team.
Reviews are unnecessarily brutal. Personal attacks and innuendo are common. Authors become defensive.	• When inappropriate comments are made, the moderators must ask that they be discontinued. • Train moderators in meeting facilitation and conflict management. • Provide all team members with training that includes practice inspections of actual team work products. • Have the review coordinator observe reviews and suggest ways that reviewers can participate more effectively. • Schedule a coaching session on effective interpersonal interactions for the group and make sure the offenders attend. Describe it as a refresher session, not as a punitive activity. • When assembling review teams, watch out for personality conflicts that could undermine the review's effectiveness. • If necessary, eject offenders from reviews or terminate the review and explain why to the process owner.

(*continued*)

Table 11–1. Symptoms and Solutions for Common Review Problems (*cont.*)

Symptoms	*Possible Solutions*
The moderator does not control the review meeting effectively.	• Select moderators who have the personality, skills, experience, and motivation to be effective. • Provide moderators with specialized training. • Have the review coordinator observe moderators in action and coach them on how to become more effective. • Remove ineffective moderators from the pool of qualified moderators.
Planning Issues	
Reviews do not appear in the project plan.	• Include reviews at designated checkpoints in all of your organization's development life-cycles. • Make sure that projects include the reviews in their schedule, activity, and resource plans. Higher management encouragement may be necessary.
Reviews are perceived to slow down the project.	• Incorporate reviews, including rework and follow-up, into the project schedule from the outset. Adding them to an existing committed schedule can indeed cause slips. • Ensure that adequate resources are allocated to support the review process. • Check whether conservative review appraisals that are holding up the project schedule are justified. If so, look for defect prevention opportunities in early life-cycle deliverables. • Check whether the reviews are effective at finding major defects. If not, they aren't adding proportionate value. • Make sure the peer review process is being followed, that reviews are not being held too early or too late, and that authors are correcting the defects found. • Emphasize the review of early life-cycle products such as requirements and designs.

(continued)

Table 11–1. Symptoms and Solutions for Common Review Problems (*cont.*)

Symptoms	Possible Solutions
	• Stress the positive impact that reviews have on testing activities. • Study lessons learned from the reviews that have been held to see if the process needs adjustment.
Reviews are skipped in a crisis or time crunch.	• Point out the risks of skipping the review, whether this is a thoughtful business decision or a knee-jerk reaction to time pressure. It will take time for the team members and managers to internalize reviews enough to realize that the project succeeds because of its quality practices, not in spite of them.
People do not review the appropriate portions of their work products.	• Have moderators work with authors to select the material most in need of review. • Provide process guidance to select the right parts of the material based on risk. • Use sampling to estimate the quality of work products and judge whether the entire document or just specific portions ought to be inspected.
Roles are not clear among the review participants.	• Verify that your organization's review process clearly defines the roles for formal reviews. • Train all review participants in the review process. • Assign roles to reviewers, with their agreement, prior to the review meeting.
Effectiveness Issues	
Review participants choose inappropriate preparation methods or analysis techniques.	• Develop analysis techniques that are suitable for the work products being reviewed. • Collect data so you know which methods are most effective. • Provide reviewers with adequate training. • Develop process guidance to suggest appropriate analysis techniques for different

(*continued*)

Table 11–1. Symptoms and Solutions for Common Review Problems (*cont.*)

Symptoms	*Possible Solutions*
	work products, review objectives, product sizes, and so on. • Have moderators assign specific preparation responsibilities and analysis techniques to individual reviewers.
Discussions during review meetings to revisit decisions made long ago or question the work product's background.	• Begin reviewing a series of related work products early in the development sequence, rather than waiting until the final deliverables are completed, so that issues are resolved and fundamental errors detected early.
Participants are not adequately prepared for review meetings.	• Ensure that all reviewers and project managers understand the importance of preparation at the prescribed rates so they treat preparation as a high-priority activity. • Deliver the materials being reviewed to all reviewers at least two or three business days prior to the meeting. • Ensure that all reviewers know how to use defect checklists, rules, and other analysis methods. • Build reviews into everyone's schedule. Check whether individuals are planning their personal schedules to accommodate preparation time. • Empower moderators to terminate review meetings if participants are not prepared. Convey the reason for the termination to the peer review process owner.
Reviews find certain kinds of defects but frequently miss others. Many defects are not caught by the reviews.	• Make sure the review process is being followed and that meetings are not turning into brainstorming or problem-solving sessions. • Use inspections instead of informal reviews. • Classify the escaping defects and identify the life-cycle activities in which they are being created. Provide training to reviewers that emphasize detecting these kinds of defects.

(*continued*)

Table 11–1. Symptoms and Solutions for Common Review Problems (*cont.*)

Symptoms	*Possible Solutions*
	• Update defect checklists and analysis methods for the corresponding deliverables to include the escaping defects. • See whether specific participants or perspectives are absent who might be able to find the types of defects that are missed.
Reviews keep finding the same kinds of defects.	• Analyze defect patterns to discover process changes that will reduce defect injection rates. • Look for other instances of the common defects throughout the project's work products of the same type. • Provide training to developers to make them aware of these kinds of defects. Stress techniques to prevent such defects and to find them earlier.
Reviews find too many defects.	• Perform an initial quick examination of work products to estimate their quality before reviewing them. Moderators can do this when checking whether the initial deliverable satisfies its review entry criteria. • Use peer deskchecks as a preliminary review method prior to holding team reviews. • Provide authors with quality tools so they can efficiently remove or prevent many defects on their own prior to review. • Ensure that authors are adequately trained to do their development work. • Make sure there is no reward process (real or perceived) in place that motivates reviewers to inflate the number of defects they report. • Use preliminary reviews after a small fraction of the work is done to correct systemic problems and reveal improvement opportunities early. • Analyze defect patterns to discover process changes that will reduce defect injection rates. *(continued)*

Table 11–1. Symptoms and Solutions for Common Review Problems (*cont.*)

Symptoms	*Possible Solutions*
Reviews find many minor, but few major defects.	• Determine how and when the major defects are ultimately being detected. • Judge whether the current checklists and analysis techniques should be able to detect such defects. If not, modify them so they will. • See whether reviewers are using the analysis techniques effectively. Provide any necessary training and practice. • See whether reviewers are preparing at the optimum rates. • Use document standards to avoid style distractions. • Use inspections instead of informal reviews.
Reviews are held too late to be effective. Excessive rework is required to correct all the review findings.	• See if authors are trying to perfect their products before submitting them for review. • Use preliminary reviews after a small fraction of the work is done to correct systemic problems and reveal improvement opportunities early enough for the author to incorporate them with modest effort.
Rework is not done correctly. Bad fixes are common.	• Perform follow-up to verify rework. • Make sure the verifiers are qualified and thorough. • Use re-review as a formal follow-up activity.

Management Issues

Management does not support peer reviews or actively opposes them.	• Educate managers about the costs and benefits of a review program. Use literature data and personal experiences. • Run some pilot reviews or inspections and present the resulting benefits and lessons to managers. • Perform reviews even if managers oppose them, because it's the professional way to build high-quality software. "Never let your boss or

(*continued*)

Table 11–1. Symptoms and Solutions for Common Review Problems (*cont.*)

Symptoms	*Possible Solutions*
	your customer talk you into doing a bad job" (Wiegers 1996a). A stealth review program is better than none.
Management does not set clear expectations for reviews.	• Have management issue a policy that clarifies the expectations. • Ask management to hold team members accountable for conforming to the policy, such as making their products available for review and participating constructively in reviews.
Management wants to participate in reviews when they should not.	• Explain the risks of having managers attend reviews. • Establish and enforce a policy that indicates that the author's first-line manager may attend only at the author's invitation and that higher-level managers may not attend reviews of their subordinates' work. • If a manager shows up uninvited and the author is not comfortable proceeding, terminate the review and explain why to the process owner. • Encourage managers to have their own work products reviewed.
Managers use metrics data inappropriately or ask to view data they are not entitled to see.	• Explain the dangers of evaluating individuals based on review data. • Include a statement in the organization's review policy that prohibits the use of inspection data for individual performance evaluation. • Ensure that metrics data from reviews is protected from inappropriate access. • If the behavior persists, stop reporting data to management. • As an extreme measure, individuals can refuse to participate in official reviews and explain why they made this decision.

(continued)

Table 11–1. Symptoms and Solutions for Common Review Problems (*cont.*)

Symptoms	*Possible Solutions*
Data collected during the review is not used for anything.	• Have management, the peer review process owner, and the peer review coordinator decide what metrics are important and how best to present the data. • Ensure that data is being reported to the peer review coordinator and that he is storing the data in a repository. • Provide suitable data analysis and reporting tools. • If appropriate, take the initiative yourself to analyze the data and disseminate reports to encourage management to do more with it. It's important to reach the point where data is collected and stored for analysis, so keep it up even if the value is minimal initially. • If the data still doesn't get used despite all these efforts, stop collecting it.

CHAPTER TWELVE

Special Review Challenges

Certain situations demand special approaches to peer reviews. Not all of these problems are easily solvable, and reviews won't succeed in every situation. Here we look at ways to address some of these challenges, including the problems of large work products, reviewers separated by time or space, reviewing generated code, too many reviewers, and a shortage of qualified reviewers.

Large Work Products

Many contemporary software applications have thousands of requirements and hundreds of thousands of lines of code, perhaps with portions written by multiple companies. You probably can't inspect all of the deliverables for such a large project, although the benefits of inspecting even huge requirements documents will likely outweigh the costs. To get the greatest return from your review investment, use risk analysis to identify the components in which undetected errors could cause the greatest future problems. Chapter 3 identified several factors that increase risk, based on the likelihood that defects will remain in the product and the potential consequences if you don't find the defects. Use formal reviews (inspections, team reviews) for the components having the greatest risk, and use informal reviews (peer deskchecks, passarounds) for the low-risk items. You might elect not to review some deliverables at all, but that should be a carefully considered business decision. Make sure the author knows which portions were not reviewed.

Sampling portions of a large work product provides an indication of its overall quality and helps you judge whether it's worth looking carefully at more than just a few pages (Gilb and Graham 1993). I often suggest that people who question the need to inspect requirements documents have several stakeholders carefully examine a random specification page from different perspectives. They will probably find so many serious problems that they will decide to inspect the entire document. If a thorough inspection of a representative sample reveals few major defects, inspecting the rest of the product might not be worthwhile.

When reviewing a large document, take a divide-and-conquer approach. Ask specific reviewers to begin their examination at different pages, rather than having only the first few pages studied with fresh eyes. However, have some overlapping coverage to provide continuity and to see whether the reviewers are finding the same defects or different types of issues. Another option is to have small groups review different portions of the document in parallel, rather than having one large team attempt to cover the whole thing. A passaround is an appropriate review technique for large documents, provided that you recognize its shortcomings, as described in Chapter 3. Ask individuals to review different parts of the product, to look for different problems (perhaps using separate portions of a defect checklist), or to use a variety of analysis methods.

Begin reviewing a large work product while it is still small. It's easy to get someone to spend 15 minutes looking at an outline or an hour examining the first section, while enlisting reviewers for a "completed" 50-page document is a challenge. I recently reviewed a badly flawed 300-page software requirements specification. It had serious organizational problems, violated every rule for writing unambiguous requirements, and omitted vital information. Had I reviewed just the first 30 pages several months ago, I could have suggested many improvements in the way the SRS was being written, which would have saved much rework at this late stage.

A fellow consultant experienced good results when each of several subteams that had produced different portions of a large design document gave its portion to a different subteam for concurrent review. Next, the entire team held a large group review to find cross-component errors. Each subteam then fixed its portion of the product. This is a way to mesh technical reviews with software construction activities. It can accelerate project completion, provided that the product is partitioned into components that separate groups can address.

Geographical or Time Separation

Increasingly, software development projects involve teams that collaborate across multiple corporations, time zones, continents, nationalities, organizational cultures, and native languages. Such projects must modify the traditional face-to-face peer review method. The review issues include both communication logistics and cultural factors; the latter pose the greater challenge. Different cultures have different attitudes toward critiquing work performed by another team member or by a supervisor. If you face such a multicultural challenge, learn about ways to get members of different cultures to collaborate, and adjust your expectations about peer reviews (Schein 1997).

Philips Semiconductors encountered cultural barriers on a project that involved collaborating development teams in Singapore and the Netherlands (Van Veenendaal 1999). Developers in Singapore were not accustomed to having others comment on their work. They could take well-meaning comments personally, especially if comments were presented semi-publicly during an inspection meeting. To deal with this cultural factor, Philips matched a coauthor from the Netherlands with each work product from Singapore and held all inspections in the Netherlands. This approach succeeded, but it sidestepped the underlying issue and essentially permitted the Singapore developers to avoid engagement in the inspections.

In an open culture, team members are accustomed to offering quality improvement suggestions to anyone, and they are receptive to suggestions from any source. In other cultures, presenting even constructive criticism to your manager is not acceptable. People from certain nations or geographical regions are comfortable with a more aggressive interaction style than are others, who avoid confrontation. A review participant from the more restrained community might feel that someone from the assertive domain is dominating the review, while an assertive participant wonders why his quiet counterpart isn't contributing to the discussion.

Some organizations are so territorial that they resist suggestions made by people outside their own community, while others are happy to have anyone catch a bug. I visited one company where it was unacceptable to point out deficiencies in your own organization's development process. You could blame the author for applying the process incorrectly, or you could criticize another organization's process. However, your own process, regardless of its shortcomings, was immune from criticism.

Table 12–1. Review Approaches for Different Participant Locations and Time Availability

	Time	
Place	**Same**	**Different**
Same	Traditional review meeting	Asynchronous review
Different	Distributed review meeting	Asynchronous review

When you plan reviews for cross-cultural development projects, be aware of these interaction differences and consider which review approaches will work best (Rothman 2001). Discuss these sensitive points with review participants to make everyone aware of how their differences will affect the review process. Hold an initial face-to-face training session to surface the cultural and communication issues so the team can determine how best to function. Thoughtful people will respect the cultural differences and will strive to make the reviews succeed.

Even if cultural barriers are not an issue, you'll need to deal with the logistical challenges of holding reviews with participants who cannot meet face-to-face. The two dimensions to consider are time and place (Table 12–1). If review participants can assemble in the same location, you can hold a traditional review meeting. Geographically separated participants can hold a distributed review meeting, while reviewers who cannot connect in real time can practice asynchronous reviews. Your collaborations will be more effective if the participants meet in person at least once early on. Use this meeting to establish the team rapport and respect for the moderator's leadership that are necessary for effective reviews. Periodic face-to-face meetings throughout the project will help maintain the bond the team members established at the beginning.

Distributed Review Meeting

Audio- and videoconferencing tools facilitate communication if the participants are available at the same time but in different places. "Same time" is complicated when the participants reside in different time zones. My colleague Erik moderated several inspections that involved six participants who spanned 12 time zones. A cultural aspect of this situation is to change the time of day that you hold the reviews to rotate the inconvenience of getting up in the middle of the night. This avoids the perception that certain individuals or locations are subordinate to others.

Distributed reviews place special burdens on both the participants and the moderator. When I participated in a distributed inspection by telephone, I was struck by the absence of body language and facial expressions. I couldn't tell what the other participants were doing or thinking. I couldn't see when someone looked puzzled or looked like he was getting ready to say something. Use expert moderators for long-distance reviews. Establish some ground rules for taking turns speaking, identifying yourself before making a comment, relinquishing control to the moderator, and timeboxing discussions to a specific maximum duration. Consultant Johanna Rothman described many conference call do's and don'ts for multicultural project meetings (Rothman 2001). A round-robin approach to raising issues can keep all participants engaged when the moderator has difficulty knowing who is not contributing.

My colleague Chris used a moderator at each of the three locations participating in a series of conference-call inspection meetings. During the meeting, each moderator facilitated the participation by the team members present in his room. The moderators conferred before and after each session to discuss which aspects worked well and which did not.

I know one moderator who uses a whistle when leading audioconference inspections. A short toot gains the attention of participants who can't see when the moderator is trying to break into the discussion. Another moderator has used the dialing beeps on the telephone as an attention-getter. A simple tone sequence such as the opening notes of Beethoven's Fifth Symphony (dial 3-3-3-7) is easily recognized.

The moderator cannot detect sidebar conversations over the telephone or see when participants have left the room or are distracted. Videoconferencing addresses some of these problems. However, the time lag in videoconference equipment can be distracting and makes it easy for multiple participants to begin speaking simultaneously. Then they all stop speaking, and the cycle begins anew. During a videoconference review, the moderator can hold up a colored piece of paper or wave a flag when he needs to get the group's attention.

Distributed reviews benefit from Internet-based collaboration tools; see Appendix B for pointers to some examples. Some of these tools display the product being reviewed in a browser-like display so all participants see the same image. An online issue log lets the recorder capture items as the reviewers bring them up, perhaps displaying the log in the browser for remote participants to view. Hyperlinks between the product under review and supporting documents permit facile navigation during the distributed discussion. Some studies of such collaborative review approaches indicate that they can be as effective as face-to-face meetings (Mashayekhi et al. 1993).

Asynchronous Review

If your reviewers can participate only in different times and places, or even at different times in the same location, use asynchronous review approaches. With the passaround technique, reviewers comment on a work product at their convenience and the author processes the accumulated comments. E-mail can serve as an asynchronous review tool, but assembling the information is tedious and evaluating the degree of agreement on issues is difficult. Asynchronous reviews address some of the potential shortcomings of traditional peer reviews: insufficient preparation, moderator domination, incorrect review rate, personality conflicts, issue resolution and meeting digression, and recording difficulties (P. Johnson 1994). The author should expect to spend some time following up on comments made by specific reviewers, which he can do face-to-face if geography permits or by telephone if it does not.

Asynchronous reviews have their own shortcomings. They require that participants contribute input over a period of time, so they can take longer to complete than real-time meetings. Some volunteers won't find the time or motivation to contribute to an asynchronous review. Asynchronous reviews lack the physical meeting that focuses the participants' attention on the problem at hand and stimulates the synergy that enhances defect discovery. The initial contributors to the discussion can set its direction if their comments are visible to all participants from the beginning. Some people don't bother to contribute when they see that someone else has already commented.

Several collaborative tools can enhance asynchronous reviewing (or even real-time inspections), although few are commercially available (Tervonen 1996). One that is, ReviewPro from Software Development Technologies, provides many features to support both asynchronous and concurrent reviews, including a threaded discussion feature to let reviewers comment on issues that are raised. Philip Johnson and his colleagues developed the Collaborative Software Review System (CSRS), available under the GNU public license (P. Johnson 1994, 1996a; P. Johnson et al. 1993). Used in conjunction with a review approach called FTArm (Formal, Technical, Asynchronous Review Method), CSRS first allows reviewers to raise private issues about the item being reviewed. Next, the tool permits them to view, respond to, and vote on issues and action proposals contributed by other reviewers. Tools such as CSRS capture more details of discussions and the thought process behind them than a recorder can note during a traditional fast-moving review meeting.

Engaging review participants in different locations or at different times is challenging. However, the benefits that distributed and asynchronous reviews contribute to collaborative software development projects make them well worth pursuing.

Generated and Nonprocedural Code

There is little point in manually reviewing code generated by graphical user interface builders, visual development tools, and the like. If you're using a code generator, you must assume that the generation proceeds correctly under all circumstances. Instead of examining the code, review the designs or other inputs that these tools used to generate the code. Errors in these higher-level work products will inevitably lead to defects in the generated code.

Maintaining generated code requires special care (Freedman 1992). Modifying the generated code directly creates a disconnect between the code and its specification, as recorded in whatever inputs you fed to the generator. If you regenerate the code in the future, perhaps because of a change to those inputs, your manual edits will be overwritten. Make changes in your project deliverables at the highest level of abstraction that the change affects, not directly in the code, and review those changes for correctness before letting the generator crank out the revised code.

Code written in nonprocedural languages such as SQL, fourth-generation query languages, or report generators tells the computer what to do but does not specify a sequence of instructions for performing the task. When you review code written in such high-level languages, check for characteristics such as these:

- The query criteria are correct.
- Relational joins are defined for maximum efficiency.
- Table indexes are used appropriately.
- The correct logic is specified for grouping, sorting, and combining retrieved data, such as when keywords GROUP BY, UNION, and DISTINCT are used in a SQL query.

Too Many Participants

A common review obstacle is that an author cannot entice anyone to review his work. Less often, more people wish to participate than is practical for an effective inspection. This happens when inspecting requirements specifications or other documents that affect many stakeholders (Wiegers 1999). Indeed, the number of project roles suggested for a requirements specification inspection in Table 5–1 exceeds the recommended limit of seven or eight inspectors. Although successful inspections involving 20 or more participants have been reported, they pose serious control problems. Such a large meeting can easily degenerate into a chaotic free-for-all. Even a well-moderated inspection with a large team will cover the material at a sluggish pace, making the inspection expensive.

I once inspected a new process document for an organization. To my surprise, 14 people arrived for the inspection meeting. We quickly discovered that 14 people have difficulty agreeing on anything. It took us three meetings to cover the material we expected to complete in a single meeting. The meetings often began late because participants continued to arrive past the appointed start time. To control late arrival, the moderator should either begin on time with the inspectors who are present or reschedule the meeting for a later time. If your managers are committed to inspections, they will want to know why meetings were postponed and will set an expectation that participants will arrive on time.

Sometimes people invite themselves to inspections for political or managerial, not technical reasons. Make sure you understand which perspective each potential participant represents, using the guidance in Table 5–1 and remembering the concerns about management and observer participation discussed in Chapter 5. Avoid duplicate points of view that add little value.

If you must deal with a large group, consider breaking it into several small teams that can work in parallel and pool their results, as in the N-fold inspections described in Chapter 4. If some people wish to attend the inspection meeting primarily to learn about the product, you could invite them to an overview meeting, have the author hold a walkthrough for them, or share the product with them in a passaround. If you still have a large inspection team, assign a capable moderator who can keep the meeting on track. The moderator can ask different inspectors to address specific sections or aspects during preparation, but a participant who has specific concerns will likely provide them, no matter what assignment he is given.

No Qualified Reviewers Available

Members of small software groups often protest that they cannot hold reviews because no one who is qualified to critique their work is available. If your group contains individuals who are the only people possessing certain technical skills, you have a risk of losing that specialized knowledge in these days of high software staff turnover. To mitigate this risk, begin holding reviews as cross-training to impart essential knowledge to other team members. Those reviewers won't help the author much initially. Gradually, though, they will become able to find defects and they'll learn new skills in the process. Inspection overview meetings will need to be more thorough than usual to get the inspectors up to speed. Including junior reviewers teaches them how to examine documents critically and inoculates them against making common mistakes in the future. Pair programming is another technique for efficiently sharing detailed knowledge between two developers.

I once hired an outstanding C++ developer, perhaps the most talented software engineer I've ever known. Bruce craved the benefits of peer review and was frustrated because there weren't any comparably experienced C++ programmers around. We eventually solved that problem by bringing in a contractor, Mike. Mike had less C++ expertise than Bruce did, but he was able to review Bruce's code effectively. Bruce also mentored Mike through reciprocal reviews. Both Bruce and Mike viewed their code reviews as valuable.

If you have isolated specialists in your team, look for suitably skilled colleagues in other departments, or even in other companies, with whom they can exchange work products. Perhaps developers with whom your team members worked at a previous job could perform peer deskchecks, provided there are no confidentiality issues or conflicts of interest. You might be able to find reviewing partners through Usenet newsgroups or other professional forums. If you truly cannot locate suitable reviewers, at least have the author perform rigorous deskchecks and use all of the available analysis and quality tools on his own work products.

Epilogue

Peer reviews are not most people's idea of a good time. They consume effort that we would prefer to spend on development activities. They demand that we focus on a colleague's work product instead of our own for a few hours. Reviews include both technical and social elements, yet software developers are typically more comfortable with the former. Reviews require us to step back from our work and our own self-image and invite others to tell us what we've done wrong. As authors, we must sometimes bite our tongues during review meetings, suppressing the natural tendency to explain our thinking and protect our egos.

On the other hand, anyone who has experienced well-conducted and effective peer reviews knows what a significant contribution they make to the quality of our work and how they enhance our individual capabilities. When I complete a body of work, I feel good, proud of what I've created. But then I remind myself that the work isn't really complete until some of my colleagues have looked it over. I've never created anything that was error-free on my own, so I'm grateful to all the people, with whom I have worked, who helped me become a better software engineer and writer. That doesn't mean I'm happy when someone suggests that I redo something I thought was finished. However, the end result is always an improvement over my first try.

Despite the obstacles, peer reviews can help any organization produce higher-quality software products more efficiently—a necessary condition for achieving business success with your software development efforts.

Peer Reviews and Process Improvement Models

Organizations that pursue systematic process improvement activities often follow an established process framework, such as maturity models developed by the Software Engineering Institute (SEI) or ISO 9000-3. The best-known frameworks are the Capability Maturity Model for Software (SW-CMM) (Paulk et al. 1995) and the Systems Engineering Capability Maturity Model (SE-CMM) (Bate et al. 1995). More recently the SEI has combined both of these models through the Capability Maturity Model Integration project to create the CMMI-SE/SW (CMU/SEI 2000a, 2000b). These process improvement models incorporate peer reviews to varying extents.

Capability Maturity Model for Software

The SW-CMM describes five levels of increasing software process capability, as shown in Table A–1 (Paulk et al. 1995). The expectation is that as organizations move to higher maturity levels, their ability to deliver high-quality products on schedule should improve. Productivity increases, estimates become more accurate, and the organizations deliver products that better meet customer needs with fewer defects. Individual practitioners develop a mindset that emphasizes continuous improvement in the way they build software. Some of these anticipated benefits have been verified in published reports (Herbsleb et al. 1994; Diaz and Sligo 1997).

Table A–1. Structure of the Capability Maturity Model for Software

Maturity Level	Name	Key Process Areas
1	Initial	(none)
2	Repeatable	Requirements Management Software Project Planning Software Project Tracking and Oversight Software Subcontract Management Software Quality Assurance Software Configuration Management
3	Defined	**Peer Reviews** Intergroup Coordination Software Product Engineering Integrated Software Management Training Program Organization Process Focus Organization Process Definition
4	Managed	Software Quality Management Quantitative Process Management
5	Optimizing	Defect Prevention Process Change Management Technology Change Management

As shown in Table A–1, each level except the first defines several *key process areas* or KPAs. These are aspects of project management or technical execution that a team must master to achieve a specific maturity level. This structure is called a *staged* model. The KPAs at Level 2 instill project management discipline into individual projects. This discipline provides the foundation for defining organization-wide development and quality processes at Level 3, including peer reviews. Each project then tailors the organization's standard process to meet its specific characteristics and needs. Level 4 emphasizes using quantitative measures to manage projects and processes, while a Level 5 organization focuses on continuous process improvement and preventing—not simply finding—defects. A peer review program contributes to this defect prevention. Even if your organization isn't attempting to climb the SW-CMM maturity ladder, you can thoughtfully apply the SW-CMM's guidance on almost any project.

Locating the Peer Reviews KPA at Level 3 of the SW-CMM doesn't mean that Level 1 organizations should not perform reviews. Indeed, a recent summary of CMM-based process assessment results found that eight percent of Level 1 and 22 percent of Level 2 organizations fully satisfied the Peer Reviews KPA (CMU/SEI 2001). Peer reviews are placed at Level 3 because an organization that has not yet established the process discipline and management commitment characteristic of Level 2 probably cannot sustain a formal peer review program. Individuals might perform reviews from time to time, but the team is unlikely to define an effective review process, properly support it, and consistently practice reviews. Of course, a development team could acquire the requisite process discipline without explicitly following the SW-CMM.

I believe that every software group should practice technical peer reviews, regardless of its CMM maturity level or whether it knows or cares about the SW-CMM. However, recognize the risk that a review program might fail unless you have laid the requisite management and cultural foundations established through CMM Level 2 practices.

Goals of the Peer Reviews Key Process Area

The SW-CMM states two to four goals for each KPA. When an organization undergoes a formal CMM-based assessment, the assessors judge to what extent the organization satisfies the goals for each KPA. To achieve a specific maturity level, the organization must demonstrate that it consistently satisfies all goals for the KPAs at that maturity level and all lower levels. The Peer Reviews KPA has two goals:

1. Peer review activities are planned.
2. Defects in the software work products are identified and removed.

The Peer Reviews KPA is one of the few with a goal that clearly states that beneficial results—removing defects—are achieved by performing the practices defined in the KPA. If your reviews do not actually find the defects that are in the reviewed work products, you cannot satisfy the second goal. You cannot satisfy the first goal if you hold only ad hoc reviews; you must plan reviews as part of your product development activities.

Activities Performed

In addition to the goals, the SW-CMM recommends several *key practices* that ordinarily lead to satisfying each KPA's goals. The Peer Reviews KPA describes three key practices in the Activities Performed category:

1. Peer reviews are planned and the plans are documented.
2. Peer reviews are performed according to a documented procedure.
3. Data on the conduct and results of the peer reviews are recorded.

A common misconception of the SW-CMM is that the organization must perform all the stated key practices to satisfy a KPA (Wiegers 1996b). In reality, the key practices provide guidelines, not requirements, for satisfying the goals. However, these three activities make good sense, whether or not your organization is striving to officially satisfy the Peer Reviews KPA. You need to plan what products you will review and build the reviews into the project schedule. As Chapter 10 described, the documented procedure identifies the steps involved in the peer reviews, describes reviewer roles, states entry and exit criteria, and incorporates defect checklists and related analysis techniques. The review data collected includes the effort spent on various review activities, the reviewed work product type and size, and defect counts (see Chapter 9).

Another misconception is that the SW-CMM requires that you perform inspections, although the Peer Reviews KPA says nothing at all about inspections. The SW-CMM leaves it up to each organization to select appropriate peer review methods. However, the three Activities Performed are consistent with the inspection process. The organization plans to hold inspections, defines how it will perform inspections and creates supporting process assets, and accumulates metrics data from the inspections conducted. Jim Fritsch (1998) provides valuable guidance for satisfying the SW-CMM's Peer Reviews KPA through an inspection program.

On the surface, performing the activities specified in the SW-CMM will achieve the goals for this KPA. However, you must also lay a foundation for the sustained performance of peer reviews. To this end, the SW-CMM recommends a set of key practices that help establish peer reviews as a standard part of the way an organization develops software products. These additional practices are grouped into four categories: Commitment to Perform, Ability to Perform, Measurement and Analysis, and Verifying Implementation.

Commitment to Perform

An organization demonstrates a serious commitment to peer reviews when senior management issues a written policy that states their expectations for the organization's performance of reviews. Without such a policy, individuals and teams might hold reviews when they believe it is appropriate, but reviews won't necessarily be ingrained into your organization's software development process. The policy typically identifies the work products that will be reviewed and states that trained review leaders, such as inspection moderators, will lead the reviews. Management demonstrates their sensitivity to the cultural factors by stating in the policy that they will not evaluate the individual performance of authors based on data gathered from reviews. A policy is meaningful only if management holds members of the organization accountable for conforming to it.

Chapter 2 described several other tangible indications of management commitment. One of the most important is building time into project schedules for peer review activities, including preparation, review meetings, and rework. Another sign of commitment is to assign to individuals the responsibility for creating, coordinating, monitoring, and improving the review process. The process owner and the peer review coordinator, whose roles were described in Chapter 10, perform most of these tasks.

Ability to Perform

The Ability to Perform category identifies prerequisites that an organization must satisfy to execute a process effectively. You can't expect your peer review program to succeed unless your team members have what they need to perform reviews effectively. The SW-CMM identifies three prerequisite key practices for peer reviews:

1. Adequate resources and funding are provided for performing peer reviews on each software work product to be reviewed.
2. Peer review leaders receive required training in how to lead peer reviews.
3. Reviewers who participate in peer reviews receive required training in the objectives, principles, and methods of peer reviews.

The necessary resources include the staff time required to plan each review, prepare the review materials, and execute the various review activities. Developing the necessary review procedures, checklists, and other process assets will also take time. Additional effort is required to collect and analyze review data and to monitor and improve the peer review process. You might need funding for travel or for collaboration tools to facilitate participation by reviewers in multiple geographical locations. In addition, the organization must provide training for review participants and leaders. A small investment in training greatly increases review effectiveness and accelerates adoption of reviews by the team members.

Measurement and Analysis

The SW-CMM's single key practice on measurement and analysis of peer reviews states that "Measurements are made and used to determine the status of the peer review activities." At the simplest level, these measurements track the number of reviews actually held compared to the number planned, the effort required, and the number of work products reviewed. Far more valuable is the collection and analysis of peer review data that was described in Chapter 9 and addressed under Activities Performed ("Data on the conduct and results of the peer reviews are recorded"). Accumulated review data enables you to quantify your quality goals for products and to establish measurable criteria for determining work product appraisals following review.

Verifying Implementation

Even with the best of intentions, software practitioners don't always follow the processes they are supposed to, in the intended manner at the appropriate times. Therefore, it's a good idea to have an external, objective observer assess how the organization is performing peer reviews. Such process verification is the province of a software quality assurance group, which should confirm that:

- The members of the organization are performing peer reviews as planned.
- Reviewers and review leaders are adequately trained.
- The defined procedures are appropriate and are followed.
- Review entry and exit criteria are used as intended.
- The required peer review data is collected and reported in a timely fashion.
- The reviews do in fact discover defects, which are then corrected.

Gaps between the intended and actual practice of peer reviews demand corrective action. The obvious possibility is actually to begin following the peer review process. Sometimes, though, the current process isn't fully practical or appropriate, which is why it isn't being practiced. In this case, the process owner takes the lead to adjust the process and make it better suit the organization's needs. The team can then begin to follow the modified process effectively. Verifying peer review implementation and performing the other key practices that the SW-CMM recommends will go a long way toward helping you establish and sustain an effective peer review program.

Systems Engineering Capability Maturity Model

Whereas the SW-CMM is a staged model, describing five discrete levels of increasing capability, the SE-CMM is a *continuous* model (Bate et al. 1995). The 18 process areas shown in Table A–2 are not grouped into maturity levels. Instead, an organization can achieve one of six *capability levels* with respect to each process area: Not Performed, Performed Informally, Planned and Tracked,

Table A–2. Process Areas of the Systems Engineering Capability Maturity Model

Process Areas
Analyze Candidate Solutions
Derive and Allocate Requirements
Evolve System Architecture
Integrate Disciplines
Integrate System
Understand Customer Needs and Expectations
Verify and Validate System
Ensure Quality
Manage Configurations
Manage Risk
Monitor and Control Technical Effort
Plan Technical Effort
Define Organization's Systems Engineering Process
Improve Organization's Systems Engineering Processes
Manage Product Line Evolution
Manage Systems Engineering Support Environment
Provide Ongoing Skills and Knowledge
Coordinate with Suppliers

Well Defined, Quantitatively Controlled, and Continuously Improving. The SE-CMM refers to peer reviews as *defect reviews*. It does not define a discrete process area for defect reviews or itemize specific expectations for how they are to be performed. Reviews and inspections are among the possible verification methods listed as part of the Verify and Validate System process area. The base practices in this process area include:

- Planning verification activities
- Defining the verification methods to be used
- Performing the verification steps
- Comparing the collected verification results with established evaluation criteria to assess the degree of success

In addition, defect reviews are called out as a characteristic of a well-defined process. Therefore, they will be used by an organization that has achieved Capability Level 3 (Well Defined) in a given process area. Defect reviews also appear in the description of Capability Level 4, Quantitatively Controlled, which observes that reviews are helpful when setting specific goals for the quality of the organization's work products.

CMMI-SE/SW

There are two different representations of the integrated CMM, which fuses systems and software engineering and ultimately will replace both the software and systems engineering CMMs. The staged representation is analogous to the structure of the SW-CMM, having five maturity levels with the 22 process areas shown in Table A–3 (CMU/SEI 2000b). In this staged representation, "Perform Peer Reviews" appears as a specific goal for the Verification process area at Level 3. In contrast, the continuous representation is analogous to the structure of the Systems Engineering CMM. The same 22 process areas that appear in the staged representation are grouped into four process area categories: Process Management, Project Management, Engineering, and Support. In the continuous representation, "Perform Peer Reviews" is again identified as a specific goal for the Verification process area within the Engineering process area category.

Table A–3. Structure of the CMMI for Systems Engineering/Software Engineering, Staged Representation

Maturity Level	Name	Process Areas
1	Initial	(none)
2	Managed	Requirements Management Project Planning Project Monitoring and Control Supplier Agreement Management Measurement and Analysis Process and Product Quality Assurance Configuration Management
3	Defined	Decision Analysis and Resolution Risk Management Integrated Product Management Organizational Training Organization Process Definition Organization Process Focus Validation Verification Product Integration Technical Solution Requirements Development
4	Quantitatively Managed	Organizational Process Performance Quantitative Project Management
5	Optimizing	Organizational Innovation and Deployment Causal Analysis and Resolution

While the CMM for Software does not specify a particular type of peer review, the CMMI-SE/SW implies that inspections are the preferred peer review technique and emphasizes their objective of defect identification. The description of "Perform Peer Reviews" is the same in both representations of the CMMI-SE/SW. It consists of three specific practices:

1. Prepare for peer reviews of selected work products.
2. Conduct peer reviews on selected work products and identify issues resulting from the peer review.
3. Analyze data about preparation, conduct, and results of the peer reviews.

A properly implemented inspection program will satisfy the "Perform Peer Reviews" goal. The Verification process area cross-references to several other process areas. These links illustrate the connections between peer reviews and Requirements Development, Product Integration, Measurement and Analysis, Project Monitoring and Control, and Technical Solution.

Prepare for Peer Reviews

Preparation activities include developing the infrastructure that enables an organization to conduct peer reviews effectively, as well as planning and preparing for individual reviews. Infrastructure development involves creating defect checklists and rule sets, developing a project's review schedule, providing training, defining data collection expectations, and defining entry, exit, and re-review criteria. Preparing for a specific review involves choosing an appropriate review type, identifying the participants and assigning roles, assessing whether the work product satisfies its entry criteria, and distributing the review package. As with inspections, having reviewers individually examine the work product prior to holding a review meeting is another aspect of preparation.

Conduct Peer Reviews

As you would expect, this practice involves actually reviewing the work product according to the selected procedure. Identified defects and issues are documented, as are the required review data. Any action items coming out of the review are communicated to the appropriate project stakeholders. If necessary, a re-review is planned to evaluate the corrections made. The review is completed when the product satisfies its exit criteria.

Analyze Peer Review Data

As with the Peer Reviews KPA in the SW-CMM, the Verification process area states that the project will "record data related to the preparation, conduct, and results of the peer reviews." The organization is expected to store the data, analyze it, and protect it from inappropriate use. Data analysis enables the organization to track its actual peer review performance against the intended performance, to judge how effectively the reviews reveal defects, and to improve its review and product development processes.

ISO 9000-3

ISO 9000-3 ("part three") presents guidelines for applying the ISO 9001 standard to software (ISO 1997). Unlike the SEI's maturity models, ISO 9000-3 does not describe specific process areas that an organization must satisfy. Instead, it specifies that a software supplier must "establish and maintain a document quality system" that pervades the product development life-cycle. Technical peer reviews are appropriate components of this quality system. For example, the standard indicates that organizations should plan and perform product design reviews according to documented procedures. Design changes are also to be reviewed. However, the ISO 9000-3 standard does not mandate that the organization perform specific types of peer reviews. It also contains far less detail about the expected conduct of peer reviews than does the SW-CMM or the CMMI-SE/SW.

Whether or not your organization chooses to use one of these frameworks as a guide for process improvement, their recommendations can help you implement a practical and effective peer review approach. Keep in mind, though, that it's far more important to begin reaping the benefits from peer reviews than to satisfy the letter of a particular process improvement model.

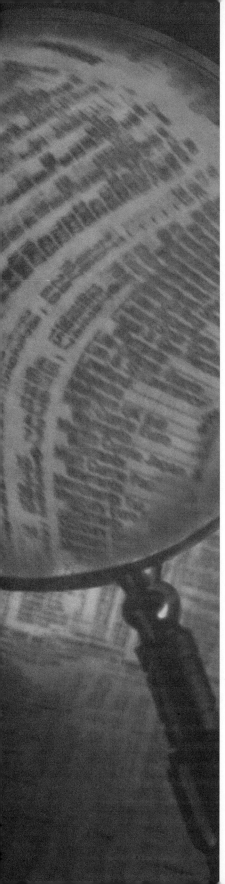

Supplemental Materials

The Web site associated with *Peer Reviews in Software: A Practical Guide* is located at *http://www.processimpact. com/pr_goodies.shtml* or by going to *http://www.awl.com/ cseng*. There you will find several items that can help you implement the practices described in this book. These items might be modified on the basis of further experience, and new items might be added from time to time. These materials are provided without warranty, express or implied, of any kind. You are welcome to use them on your own projects, modify them to best suit your needs, and share them with your colleagues, but you may not sell or license them to any third party.

Work Aids

The following documents are available for downloading at the time of writing:

- Forms used in an inspection, including the inspection summary report, inspection issues log, and typo list
- Inspection moderator's checklist
- Inspection Lessons Learned questionnaire
- Sample peer review process description
- Defect checklists for various kinds of software work products
- Inspection data collection spreadsheets

Other Peer Review Resources

Hyperlinks are provided to providers of training on inspections and inspection moderation. Links are also provided to information about commercial and free tools that can support the review process and to tools that analyze source code and other documents for problems. Additional links point to sources of useful information on peer reviews, including extensive bibliographies of publications on software inspections. Every attempt will be made to keep the links from this Web site to the other sources of information current, but Web links are notoriously volatile. Please report any broken links to me at kwiegers@acm.org or to the publisher of this book.

Glossary of Peer Review Terms

ad hoc review: A type of informal review in which a practitioner spontaneously asks a colleague to help find a problem in a component under development.

appraisal: The collective judgment of an inspection team as to the quality of the product being inspected. Includes a decision as to what type of rework verification is required during the inspection follow-up stage.

asynchronous review: A peer review in which reviewers contribute comments independently at various times without holding a meeting.

author: The individual who created or maintains a work product that is being reviewed.

baseline: A document, program, or other work product that has been agreed upon or approved at a specific point in time as a foundation for subsequent development work.

causal analysis: An inspection stage in which the participants seek to understand the root cause of each defect found and identify ways to prevent future occurrences of similar defects.

checklist: See *defect checklist.*

control chart: A graph of observations from individual executions of a process that shows the stability of the process over time.

data item: An attribute of a software component or process that can be measured or counted directly, such as preparation effort, product size, and defect counts.

decision rule: A rule or technique that a group of people apply to reach a collective decision on an issue. Possibilities include majority vote, consensus, unanimity, spontaneous agreement, and delegation of the decision to a single individual.

defect: A condition in a software work product that would cause the software to produce an unsatisfactory or unexpected result; also known as a bug or fault.

defect checklist: A categorized list of the kinds of defects that are typically found in a specific type of work product.

defect containment: The fraction of defects that are detected in the same life-cycle phase in which they were created.

defect density: The number of defects found per unit (pages or thousand lines of code) of work product reviewed.

defect log: See *issue log.*

deliverable: An interim or final document, program, file, or other artifact created during the execution of an engineering project. Used in this book as a synonym for "work product."

dynamic analysis: The use of defect removal techniques that evaluate the behavior of software during execution. Examples include testing and the use of automated tools that detect run-time errors.

dysfunction: See *measurement dysfunction.*

effectiveness: See *inspection effectiveness.*

efficiency: See *inspection efficiency.*

entry criteria: Conditions that must be satisfied before a process, such as an inspection, can be executed with confidence of success.

error: A mistake made while creating or modifying a work product that leads to the introduction of a defect.

exit criteria: Conditions that must be satisfied to declare that an execution of a process, such as an inspection, was successfully completed.

follow-up: An inspection stage in which someone designated by the moderator examines the author's rework to ensure that it was performed correctly and that all open issues were satisfactorily resolved.

formal review: A peer review that has most or all of the following characteristics: defined objectives, participation by a trained team, leadership by a trained moderator, specific participant roles and responsibilities, a documented review procedure, reporting of results to management, explicit entry and exit criteria, tracking defects to closure, and recording process and quality data. Examples are inspection and team review.

informal review: A peer review that lacks many of the characteristics of a formal review. Examples are ad hoc review, pair programming, peer deskcheck, and passaround.

injection rate: The number of defects per unit size (page or thousand lines of code) that are created in a work product during its development.

inspection: A type of formal peer review that incorporates multiple process stages, including a meeting, and in which people other than the author of the work product lead the review and describe the work product to the rest of the review team.

inspection effectiveness: The percentage of the defects originally present in a work product that was detected by inspection.

inspection efficiency: The average number of defects discovered per labor hour of inspection effort.

inspection package: A set of materials that the author and moderator deliver to the inspectors prior to the inspection meeting. Includes the work product being inspected and possibly predecessor documents that define its specifications, as well as pertinent standards, necessary forms, checklists or rule sets, and/or test documentation for the work product.

inspection summary report: A report that identifies the work product that was inspected, the inspection participants and their roles, the work product appraisal, and data about the inspection's duration and effort consumption.

inspector: A person who examines a work product for defects in an inspection. Might also perform one of the specialized inspection roles of reader, recorder, or moderator. The work product's author is also an inspector.

issue: An item brought up during an inspection that is not known to be a defect but which requires attention from the author. Examples include questions, points of style, and points that need clarifying.

issue log: A list of possible defects, improvement suggestions, and other issues that inspectors identified during or prior to the inspection meeting; also called a defect log or defect list.

major defect: A fault in a work product that could have a severe impact on the product's correct functioning and would likely be much more expensive or difficult to correct if found late in the product's development cycle than if found early.

measurement dysfunction: A situation in which measurement of a process leads to an undesired outcome because people change their behavior to make the measurement yield a favorable result or to avoid being penalized for their results.

metric: A value that quantifies a given attribute of a software component or process. The metric is derived from one or more data items measured directly from the component or process. Examples include defect density and preparation rate.

minor defect: A fault in a work product that would not cause severe consequences for the user and would not be substantially more expensive to correct if it is found late in the product's development cycle than if found early.

moderator: The individual who leads an inspection or other formal review; also called the review leader. Responsible for planning the events with the author, scheduling and facilitating meetings, collecting and reporting measurements from inspections he moderates, and possibly verifying the author's rework. The author may not perform this role.

N-fold inspection: The use of several small teams to inspect the same work product independently.

observer: Someone who attends an inspection meeting but does not examine the product being inspected for defects.

origin: The life-cycle activity during which a defect was initially injected into a work product.

overview: An inspection stage in which the author presents the other inspectors with background information on the work product being inspected so they can adequately prepare for the inspection meeting.

pair programming: A software development practice in which two people write code collaboratively, using a single workstation, continuously reviewing and improving their joint work. Constitutes a type of informal peer review.

passaround: A type of informal peer review in which the author of a work product asks several other people to examine it independently for possible defects.

peer deskcheck: A type of informal peer review in which the author of a work product asks one other person to examine it for possible defects.

peer review: An activity in which one or more persons other than the author of a work product examine that product with the intent of finding defects and improvement opportunities.

peer review coordinator: An individual who manages and analyzes data collected from an organization's peer reviews, coaches reviewers and moderators, schedules and possibly presents training sessions, and works with the peer review

process owner to make a review program effective.

preparation: An inspection stage in which inspectors examine the deliverable being inspected on their own to understand it and identify possible defects.

process assets library: A collection of process descriptions, procedures, templates, forms, checklists, and other work aids to assist an organization's successful performance of its defined development and quality processes.

process owner: A manager or senior process engineer who oversees an organization's peer review program, serves as an advocate, and provides a contact point for incorporating improvements in the review process.

reader: An inspection participant who describes the product being inspected to the other inspectors during the inspection meeting; also called the presenter. The author may not perform this role.

recorder: An inspection participant who documents the defects and issues brought up during the inspection meeting on the issue log; also called the scribe. The author may not perform this role.

return on investment: The net savings from an inspection program (based on prevented rework) divided by the cost of the inspection program.

review: One of several types of activities in which a group of people examine artifacts produced on a software or other engineering project. Used in this book as a synonym for "peer review."

rework: An inspection stage in which the author, and perhaps others, correct defects found in the inspected work product and in any associated or previous work products.

rule: A statement or standard that directs authors to perform tasks or construct product documents in a particular way. Might address document contents, structure, conventions, or notations.

severity: An indication of the likely impact that a defect discovered during a peer review would have had on the correct functioning of the software product.

software engineering process group: A team that leads and coordinates the process improvement activities in a software development organization.

static analysis: The use of defect removal techniques performed on source code or other software components that do not involve execution of the software. Examples include peer review and the use of automated tools that detect syntax or construction errors.

test case: A set of specific conditions, actions, and expected results that describe one aspect of how a software product should behave.

testing: The execution of software under specified conditions to judge whether its behavior conforms to the expected results.

type: For items found during a peer review, a code that indicates what kind of issue or defect each item is, according to a classification scheme selected by the development organization.

typo list: A list of typographical, cosmetic, and other minor errors that an inspector found during individual preparation. Items on the typo list are not discussed in the inspection meeting.

validation: The process of evaluating a work product to determine whether it satisfies customer requirements.

verification: The process of evaluating a work product to determine whether it satisfies the specifications and conditions imposed on it at the beginning of the development phase during which it was created.

verifier: The individual who checks the changes made in an inspected work product. Could be the moderator, a quality engineer, or someone else designated by the moderator.

walkthrough: A type of informal peer review in which the author of a work product describes the product to the reviewers and solicits comments on it.

work product: A document, program, or other artifact produced during the course of developing an engineering product. Could be an interim or final project deliverable or a supporting document that enables the project to be completed successfully. Examples include various types of project plans, requirements specifications, design documents, user interface designs, source code, test documentation, user and system documentation, training materials, and process documentation.

References

Ackerman, A. Frank, Lynne S. Buchwald, and Frank H. Lewski. 1989. Software Inspections: An Effective Verification Process. *IEEE Software* 6, no. 3: 31–36.

Allott, Stephen K. 1999. The Seven Habits of Highly Effective Inspection Teams. 1999. *Proceedings of the 17th Pacific Northwest Software Quality Conference.* Available at http://www.pnsqc.org/proceedings/pnsqc99/pnsqc99.pdf

Austin, Robert D. 1996. *Measuring and Managing Performance in Organizations.* New York: Dorset House Publishing.

Bankes, Kirk, and Fred Sauer. 1995. Ford systems inspection experiences. *Proceedings of the 1995 International Information Technology Quality Conference.* Orlando, Florida: Quality Assurance Institute.

Barnard, Jack, and Art Price. 1994. Managing Code Inspection Information. *IEEE Software* 11, no. 2: 59–69.

Basili, Victor R., and H. Dieter Rombach. 1988. The TAME Project: Towards Improvement-Oriented Software Environments. *IEEE Transactions on Software Engineering* 14, no. 6: 758–73.

Basili, V., S. Green, O. Laitenberger, F. Lanubile, F. Shull, S. Soerumgaard, and M. Zelkowitz. 1996. The Empirical Investigation of Perspective-Based Reading. *Empirical Software Engineering: An International Journal* 1, no. 2: 133–64.

Bass, Len, Paul Clements, and Rick Kazman. 1998. *Software Architecture in Practice.* Reading, Massachusetts: Addison-Wesley.

Bate, Roger et al. 1995. A Systems Engineering Capability Maturity Model, Version 1.1. *Technical Report CMU/SEI-95-MM-003.* Pittsburgh, Pennsylvania: Carnegie Mellon University/Software Engineering Institute.

Beck, Kent. 2000. *Extreme Programming Explained: Embrace Change.* Boston, Massachusetts: Addison-Wesley.

Beizer, Boris. 1990. *Software Testing Techniques.* 2nd edition. New York: Van Nostrand Reinhold.

Bianco, Nicole. 1996. Inspections DO NOT Work! *Software QA* 3, no. 6: 10–12.

Bias, Randolph. 1991. Walkthroughs: Efficient Collaborative Testing. *IEEE Software* 8, no. 5: 94–95.

Bisant, David B., and James R. Lyle. 1989. A Two-Person Inspection Method to Improve Programming Productivity. *IEEE Transactions on Software Engineering* 15, no. 10: 1294–1304.

Boehm, Barry W. 1981. *Software Engineering Economics.* Englewood Cliffs, New Jersey: Prentice-Hall.

Boehm, Barry, and Victor R. Basili. 2001. Software Defect Reduction Top 10 List. *IEEE Computer* 34, no. 1: 135–137.

Booch, Grady, James Rumbaugh, and Ivar Jacobson. 1999. *The Unified Modeling Language User Guide.* Reading, Massachusetts: Addison-Wesley.

Bouldin, Barbara M. 1989. *Agents of Change: Managing the Introduction of Automated Tools.* New York: Yourdon Press.

Bourgeois, Karen V. 1996. Process Insights from a Large-Scale Software Inspections Data Analysis. *CrossTalk* 9, no. 10: 17–23.

Bridge, Norman, and Corinne Miller. 1998. Orthogonal Defect Classification Using Defect Data to Improve Software Development. *Software Quality* No. 3: 1–8.

Brown, Norm. 1996. Industrial-Strength Management Strategies. *IEEE Software* 13, no. 4: 94–103.

Brykczynski, Bill. 1994. Why Isn't Inspection Used. Available from http://www2.ics.hawaii.edu/~johnson/FTR/Bib/Brykczynski94a.html

Caputo, Kim. 1998. *CMM Implementation Guide: Choreographing Software Process Improvement.* Reading, Massachusetts: Addison-Wesley.

Carnegie Mellon University/Software Engineering Institute. 2000. CMMI for Systems Engineering/Software Engineering, Version 1.02: Continuous Representation. *Technical Report CMU/SEI-2000-TR-029.* Pittsburgh, Pennsylvania: Carnegie Mellon University/Software Engineering Institute.

———. 2000. CMMI for Systems Engineering/Software Engineering, Version 1.02: Staged Representation. *Technical Report CMU/SEI-2000-TR-018.* Pittsburgh, Pennsylvania: Carnegie Mellon University/Software Engineering Institute.

———. 2001. *Process Maturity Profile of the Software Community 2000 Year End Update.* Pittsburgh, Pennsylvania: Carnegie Mellon University/Software Engineering Institute.

Chillarege, Ram, Inderpal S. Bhandari, Jarir K. Chaar, Michael J. Halliday, Diane S. Moebus, Bonnie K. Ray, and Man Yuen Wong. 1992. Orthogonal Defect Classification—A Concept for In-Process Measurements. *IEEE Transactions on Software Engineering* 18, no. 11: 943–956.

Constantine, Larry L. 1993. Work Organization: Paradigms for Project Management and Organization. *Communications of the ACM* 36, no. 10: 35–43.

Constantine, Larry L., and Lucy A. D. Lockwood. 1999. *Software for Use: A Practical Guide to the Models and Methods of Usage-Centered Design.* Reading, Massachusetts: Addison-Wesley.

Cooper, Kenneth G., and Thomas W. Mullen. 1993. Swords and Plowshares: The Rework Cycles of Defense and Commercial Software Development Projects. *American Programmer* 6, no. 5: 41–51.

Crosby, Philip B. 1979. *Quality is Free.* New York: McGraw-Hill.

Cusumano, Michael A., and Richard W. Selby. 1995. *Microsoft Secrets: How the World's Most Powerful Software Company Creates Technology, Shapes Markets, and Manages People.* New York: The Free Press.

Deimel, Lionel E. 1991. Scenes of Software Inspections: Video Dramatizations for the Classroom. *Technical Report CMU/SEI-91-EM-5.* Pittsburgh, Pennsylvania: Carnegie Mellon University/Software Engineering Institute.

Diaz, Michael, and Joseph Sligo. 1997. How Software Process Improvement Helped Motorola. *IEEE Software* 14, no. 5: 75–81.

Doolan, E. P. 1992. Experience with Fagan's Inspection Method. *Software–Practice and Experience* 22, no. 2: 173–82.

Drabick, Rodger D. 1999. On-Track Requirements. *Software Testing & Quality Engineering,* 1, no. 3: 54–60.

Dy, Bernard. 2001. Airware. *Aviation History* 11, no. 3: 74.

Ebenau, Robert G. 1994. Predictive Quality Control with Software Inspections. *CrossTalk* 7, no. 6: 9–16.

Ebenau, Robert G., and Susan H. Strauss. 1994. *Software Inspection Process.* New York: McGraw-Hill.

Fagan, M. E. 1976. Design and Code Inspections to Reduce Errors in Program Development. *IBM Systems J.* 15, no. 3: 182–211.

Fagan, Michael E. 1986. Advances in Software Inspections. *IEEE Transactions on Software Engineering* 12, no. 7: 744–51.

Florac, William A., Anita D. Carleton, and Julia R. Barnard. 2000. Statistical Process Control: Analyzing a Space Shuttle Onboard Software Process. *IEEE Software* 17, no. 4: 97–106.

Freedman, Daniel. 1992. The Devil is in the Details: Everything Important Must be Reviewed. *American Programmer* 5, no. 2: 9–13.

Freedman, Daniel P., and Gerald M. Weinberg. 1990. *Handbook of Walkthroughs, Inspections, and Technical Reviews.* 3rd edition. New York: Dorset House Publishing.

Fritsch, Jim. 1998. Formal Inspection Best-in-Class Model. *Software Quality,* No. 1: 1–6.

Genuchten, Michiel van, Cor van Dijk, Henk Scholten, and Doug Vogel. 2001. Using Group Support Systems for Software Inspections. *IEEE Software* 18, no. 3: 60–65.

Gilb, Tom. 1998. Optimizing Software Inspections. *CrossTalk* 11, no. 3: 16–19.

———. 2000. Planning to Get the Most out of Inspection. *Software Quality Professional* 2, no. 2: 7–19.

Gilb, Tom, and Dorothy Graham. 1993. *Software Inspection.* Wokingham, England: Addison-Wesley.

Gottesdiener, Ellen. 2001. Decide How to Decide. *Software Development* 9, no. 1: 65–70.

Grady, Robert B. 1992. *Practical Software Metrics for Project Management and Process Improvement.* Englewood Cliffs, New Jersey: Prentice Hall.

———. 1997. *Successful Software Process Improvement.* Upper Saddle River, New Jersey: Prentice Hall PTR.

———. 1999. An Economic Release Decision Model: Insights into Software Project Management. *Proceedings of Applications of Software Measurement '99 Conference.* San Jose, California: 225–239.

Grady, Robert B., and Tom Van Slack. 1994. Key Lessons in Achieving Widespread Inspection Use. *IEEE Software* 11, no. 4: 46–57.

Haley, Thomas J. 1996. Software Process Improvement at Raytheon. *IEEE Software* 13, no. 6: 33-41.

Harding, John T. 1998. Using Inspection Data to Forecast Test Defects. *CrossTalk* 11, no. 5: 19–24.

Herbsleb, James, David Zubrow, Jane Siegel, James Rozum, and Anita Carleton. 1994. Software Process Improvement: State of the Payoff. *American Programmer* 7, no. 9: 2–12.

Holland, Dick. 1999. Document Inspection as an Agent of Change. *Software Quality Professional* 2, no. 1: 22–33.

Hollocker, Charles P. 1990. *Software Reviews and Audits Handbook.* New York: John Wiley & Sons.

Humphrey, Watts S. 1989. *Managing the Software Process.* Reading, Massachusetts: Addison-Wesley.

———. 1995. *A Discipline for Software Engineering.* Reading, Massachusetts: Addison-Wesley.

———. 2001. Why Don't They Practice What We Preach? Carnegie Mellon University. Available at http://www.sei.cmu.edu/publications/articles/practice-preach/practice-preach.html

IEEE Std 730-1998. 1999. IEEE Standard for Software Quality Assurance Plans. *IEEE Standards Software Engineering, 1999 Edition. Volume 2: Process Standards.* New York: The Institute of Electrical and Electronics Engineers, Inc.

IEEE Std 1028-1997. 1999. IEEE Standard for Software Reviews. *IEEE Standards Software Engineering, 1999 Edition. Volume 2: Process Standards.* New York: The Institute of Electrical and Electronics Engineers, Inc.

IEEE Std 1044.1-1995. 1999. IEEE Guide to Classification for Software Anomalies. *IEEE Standards Software Engineering, 1999 Edition. Volume 4: Resource and Technique Standards.* New York: The Institute of Electrical and Electronics Engineers, Inc.

Iisakka, Juha, Ilkka Tervonen, and Lasse Harjumaa. 1999. Experiences of Painless Improvements in Software Inspection. In *Project Control for Software Quality.* Rob Kusters, Adrian Cowderoy, Fred Heemstra, and Erik van Veenendaal, eds. *Proceedings of the Combined 10th European Software Control and Metrics Conference and the 2nd SCOPE Conference on Software Product Evaluation (April 27–29, 1999),* Herstmonceux, England. Maastricht, The Netherlands: Shaker Publishing.

International Organization for Standardization (ISO). 1997. *Quality Management and Quality Assurance Standards—Part 3: Guidelines for the Application of ISO 9001 to the Development, Supply and Maintenance of Software.* Geneva, Switzerland: International Organization for Standardization.

Jalote, Pankaj. 2000. *CMM in Practice: Processes for Executing Software Projects at Infosys.* Boston, Massachusetts: Addison-Wesley.

Jeffries, Ron, Ann Anderson, and Chet Hendrickson. 2001. *Extreme Programming Installed.* Boston, Massachusetts: Addison-Wesley.

Johnson, Mark. 1994. Dr. Boris Beizer on Software Testing: An Interview. Part 1. *The Software QA Quarterly* 1, no. 2: 7–13.

Johnson, Philip M. 1994. An Instrumented Approach to Improving Software Quality Through Formal Technical Review. *Proceedings of the 16th International Conference on Software Engineering*: 113-122. Reprinted in Wheeler, David A., Bill Brykczynski, and Reginald N. Meeson, Jr. 1996. *Software Inspection: An Industry Best Practice.* Los Alamitos, California: IEEE Computer Society Press.

———. 1996. Design for Instrumentation: High Quality Measurement of Formal Technical Review. *Software Quality Journal* 5, no. 3: 33–51.

———. 1996. Measurement Dysfunction in Formal Technical Review. *ICS Technical Report 96-16.* University of Hawaii. Available from http://csdl.ics.hawaii.edu/tech reports/96-16/96-16.html.

———. 1998. Reengineering Inspection. *Communications of the ACM* 41, no. 2: 49–52.

Johnson, Philip M., Danu Tjahjono, Dadong Wan, and Robert S. Brewer. 1993. Experiences with CSRS: An Instrumented Software Review Environment. *Proceedings of the Pacific Northwest Software Quality Conference.*

Jones, C. L. 1985. A Process-Integrated Approach to Defect Prevention. *IBM Systems J.* 24, no. 2: 150-67.

Jones, Capers. 1986. *Programming Productivity.* New York: McGraw-Hill.

———. 1996. *Applied Software Measurement: Assuring Productivity and Quality.* 2nd edition. New York: McGraw-Hill.

———. 1997. *Software Quality: Analysis and Guidelines for Success.* Boston, Massachusetts: International Thomson Computer Press.

———. 2000. *Software Assessments, Benchmarks, and Best Practices.* Boston, Massachusetts: Addison-Wesley.

Kaplan, Craig A. 1995. Secrets of software quality. *Proceedings of the Fifth International Conference on Software Quality.* Austin, Texas. American Society for Quality Control: 15–27.

Kerth, Norman L. 2001. *Project Retrospectives: A Handbook for Team Reviews.* New York: Dorset House Publishing.

Knight, John C., and E. Ann Myers. 1993. An Improved Inspection Technique. *Communications of the ACM* 36, no. 11: 51–61.

Knuth, Donald E. 1992. *Literate Programming.* Stanford, California: CSLI Publications.

Lee, Earl. 1997. Software Inspections: How to Diagnose Problems and Improve the Odds of Organizational Acceptance. *CrossTalk* 10, no. 8: 10–13.

Litton Industries. 2000. Process Owners Responsibilities, V4. Systems and Process Engineering. McLean, Virginia: Litton Industries PRC.

Madachy, R. 1995. Process Improvement Analysis of a Corporate Inspection Program. *Proceedings of the Seventh Software Engineering Process Group Conference.* Boston, Massachusetts.

Mah, Michael. 2001. Defect Metrics, Inspections, and Testing: Part II. *IT Metrics Strategies* 7, no. 2: 1, 6–16.

Martin, Johnny, and W. T. Tsai. 1990. N-fold Inspection: A Requirements Analysis Technique. *Communications of the ACM* 33, no. 2: 225–232.

Mashayekhi, Vahid, Janet M. Drake, Wei-Tek Tsai, and John Riedl. 1993. Distributed, Collaborative Software Inspection. *IEEE Software* 10, no. 5: 66–75.

Mashayekhi, Vahid, Chris Feulner, and John Riedl. 1994. CAIS: Collaborative Asynchronous Inspection of Software. *Proceedings of the ACM SIGSOFT '94 Symposium on the Foundations of Software Engineering.* New Orleans, Louisiana: 21–34.

McConnell, Steve. 1996. *Rapid Development: Taming Wild Software Schedules.* Redmond, Washington: Microsoft Press.

Naccache, Nabil, and Zarrin Ghaemi. 1999. Metrics as a Process Improvement Tool. *Proceedings of the International Conference on IT Quality.* Orlando, Florida: Quality Assurance Institute.

National Aeronautics and Space Administration. 1993. Software Formal Inspections Guidebook. NASA-GB-A302.

Nielsen, Jakob. 1993. *Usability Engineering.* Boston, Massachusetts: Academic Press.

Nielsen, Jakob, and Robert L. Mack, eds. 1994. *Usability Inspection Methods.* New York: John Wiley & Sons.

O'Neill, Don. 1996. National Software Quality Experiment: Results 1992–1995. *Proceedings of the Eighth Annual Software Technology Conference,* Salt Lake City, Utah. Hill Air Force Base, Utah: Software Technology Support Center.

———. 1997. Setting Up a Software Inspection Program. *CrossTalk* 10, no. 2: 11–13.

———. 2001. Peer Reviews. In the *Encyclopedia of Software Engineering.* 2nd edition. John J. Marciniak, ed. New York: John Wiley & Sons.

Parnas, D. L., and D. M. Weiss. 1985. Active Design Reviews: Principles and Practices. *Proceedings, Eighth International Conference on Software Engineering:* 132–136.

Paulk, Mark et al. 1995. *The Capability Maturity Model: Guidelines for Improving the Software Process.* Reading, Massachusetts: Addison-Wesley.

Porter, Adam A., and Philip M. Johnson. 1997. Assessing Software Review Meetings: Results of a Comparative Analysis of Two Experimental Studies. *IEEE Transactions on Software Engineering* 23, no. 3: 129–45.

Porter, Adam, and Lawrence Votta. 1997. What Makes Inspections Work? *IEEE Software* 14, no. 6: 99–102.

Porter, Adam A., Lawrence G. Votta, Jr., and Victor R. Basili. 1995. Comparing Detection Methods for Software Requirements Inspections: A Replicated Experiment. *IEEE Transactions on Software Engineering* 21, no. 6: 563–75.

Radice, Ronald A. 2001. *Software Inspections: Past, Present, and Future.* Andover, Massachusetts: Paradoxicon Publishing.

Rothman, Johanna. 2001. Managing Multicultural Projects with Complementary Practices. *Cutter IT Journal* 14, no. 4: 7–15.

Russell, Glen W. 1991. Experience with Inspection in Ultralarge-Scale Developments. *IEEE Software* 8, no. 1: 25–31.

Sandahl, K., O. Blomkvist, J. Karlsson, C. Krysander, M. Lindvall, and N. Ohlsson. 1998. An Extended Replication of an Experiment for Assessing Methods for Software Requirements Inspections. *Empirical Software Engineering, An International Journal* 3, no. 4: 327–354.

Schein, Edgar H. 1997. *Organizational Culture and Leadership.* 2nd edition. San Francisco, California: Jossey-Bass.

Schneider, G. Michael, Johnny Martin, and W. T. Tsai. 1992. An Experimental Study of Fault Detection in User Requirements Documents. *ACM Transactions on Software Engineering and Methodology* 1, no. 2: 188–204.

Shull, Forrest, Ioana Rus, and Victor Basili. 2000. How Perspective-Based Reading Can Improve Requirements Inspections. *IEEE Computer* 33, no. 7: 73–79.

Software Quality Engineering. 1995. *High-Impact™ Inspections Seminar Notebook, Version 5.3.* Jacksonville, Florida: Software Quality Engineering.

———. 1995. *Technical Reviews & Inspections Seminar Notebook, Version 4.1.* Jacksonville, Florida: Software Quality Engineering.

Stutzke, Richard D. 1999. Measuring Defect Containment in Software Processes. In *Project Control for Software Quality.* Rob Kusters, Adrian Cowderoy, Fred Heemstra, and Erik van Veenendaal, eds. *Proceedings of the Combined 10th European Software Control and Metrics Conference and the 2nd SCOPE Conference on Software Product Evaluation,* Herstmonceux, England. Maastricht, The Netherlands: Shaker Publishing.

Tervonen, Ilkka. 1996. Support for Quality-Based Design and Inspection. *IEEE Software* 13, no. 1: 44–54.

Tripp, Leonard L., William F. Struck, and Bryan K. Pflug. 1991. The Application of Multiple Team Inspections on a Safety-Critical Software Standard. *Proc. 4th Software Eng. Standards Application Workshop.* Los Alamitos, California: IEEE Computer Society Press.

Van Veenendaal, Erik P. W. M. 1999. Practical Quality Assurance for Embedded Software. *Software Quality Professional* 1, no. 3: 7–18.

Votta Jr., Lawrence G. 1993. Does Every Inspection Need a Meeting? *Proceedings of the First ACM SIGSOFT Symposium on Software Development Engineering.* New York: ACM Press: 107–14.

Weinberg, Gerald M. 1997. *Quality Software Management, Volume 4: Anticipating Change.* New York: Dorset House Publishing.

———. 1998. *The Psychology of Computer Programming, Silver Anniversary Edition.* New York: Dorset House Publishing.

———. 2000. Where Should Moderators Come From? Available from http://www.stickyminds.com/sitewide.asp?ObjectId=2139&ObjectType=ART&Function=edetail

Weller, Edward F. 1993. Lessons from Three Years of Inspection Data. *IEEE Software* 10, no. 5: 38–45.

———. 1994. Using Metrics to Manage Software Projects. *IEEE Computer* 27, no. 9: 27–33.

———. 2000. Practical Applications of Statistical Process Control. *IEEE Software* 17, no. 3: 48–55.

Wheeler, David A., Bill Brykczynski, and Reginald N. Meeson, Jr. 1996. Peer Review Processes Similar to Inspection. In Wheeler, David A., Bill Brykczynski, and Reginald N. Meeson, Jr. *Software Inspection: An Industry Best Practice.* Los Alamitos, California: IEEE Computer Society Press.

———. 1996. *Software Inspection: An Industry Best Practice.* Los Alamitos, California: IEEE Computer Society Press.

Wiegers, Karl E. 1996. *Creating a Software Engineering Culture.* New York: Dorset House Publishing.

———. 1996. Misconceptions of the CMM. *Software Development* 4, no. 11: 57–64.

———. 1998. The Seven Deadly Sins of Software Reviews. *Software Development* 6, no. 3: 44–47.

———. 1999. *Software Requirements.* Redmond, Washington: Microsoft Press.

Williams, Laurie A., and Robert R. Kessler. 2000. All I Really Need to Know about Pair Programming I Learned in Kindergarten. *Communications of the ACM* 43, no. 5: 108–114.

Williams, Laurie, Robert R. Kessler, Ward Cunningham, and Ron Jeffries. 2000. Strengthening the Case for Pair Programming. *IEEE Software* 17, no. 4: 19–25.

Yourdon, Edward. 1989. *Structured Walkthroughs.* 4th edition. New York: Yourdon Press.

Zahran, Sami. 1998. *Software Process Improvement: Practical Guidelines for Business Success.* Harlow, England: Addison-Wesley.

Index

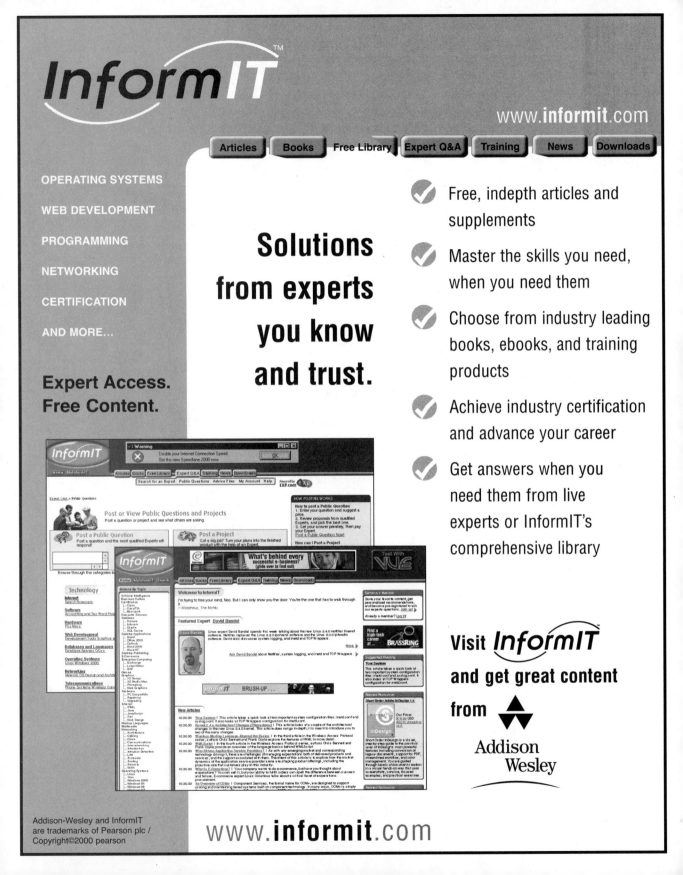

Register Your Book

at www.aw.com/cseng/register

You may be eligible to receive:
- Advance notice of forthcoming editions of the book
- Related book recommendations
- Chapter excerpts and supplements of forthcoming titles
- Information about special contests and promotions throughout the year
- Notices and reminders about author appearances, tradeshows, and online chats with special guests

Contact us

If you are interested in writing a book or reviewing manuscripts prior to publication, please write to us at:

Editorial Department
Addison-Wesley Professional
75 Arlington Street, Suite 300
Boston, MA 02116 USA
Email: AWPro@aw.com

Addison-Wesley

Visit us on the Web: http://www.aw.com/cseng